The New Dramathemes

3rd edition

Larry Swartz

Pembroke Publishers Limited

In memory of Sue Checkeris

~ For the teaching, the books, and the laughter ~

© **2002 Pembroke Publishers**
538 Hood Road
Markham, Ontario, Canada L3R 3K9
www.pembrokepublishers.com

Distributed in the U.S. by Stenhouse Publishers
477 Congress Street
Portland, ME 04101
www.stenhouse.com

We acknowledge the financial support of the Government of Canada through the Book Publishing Industry Development Program (BPIDP) for our publishing activities.

National Library of Canada Cataloguing in Publication Data

Swartz, Larry
    New dramathemes

3rd ed.
Previous eds. published under title: Dramathemes.
Includes bibliographical references and index.
ISBN 1-55138-141-9

    1. Drama—Study and teaching (Elementary) 2. Drama in education.
3. Language arts (Elementary)   I. Title. II. Title: Dramathemes

PN3171.S92 2002   372.66   C2001-904111-X

Editor: Kate Revington
Cover Design: John Zehethofer
Cover Photo: Photo Disk
Typesetting: Jay Tee Graphics Ltd.
Author Photo: Roberto Melas

Printed and bound in Canada
9 8 7 6

Contents

Acknowledgments

To:

- The children in my classroom in the Peel District Board of Education who taught me for the past twenty-five years
- The enthusiastic teachers I meet each summer and winter in the Additional Qualification courses at OISE/UT
- The teachers of tomorrow whom I guide (and who guide me) in the preservice program
- Colleagues and friends in the elementary program at OISE/UT
- Pat Shaughnessy and Eleanor Adam and the fourth and twelfth floor staffs who help me to organize and care for the courses in dramatic arts
- Kathy Broad, Brian Crawford, Jim Hewitt, Cathy Marks Krpan, and Susan Schwartz for the conversations and friendship
- Clare Kosnick, for her support and faith
- Lynn Slotkin, the goddess of theatregoers and my oldest friend
- Jonothan Neelands, Tony Goode, Warwick Dobson, and Cecily O'Neill for the insights and the learning
- My special team of course instructors who enrich the Additional Qualification courses and give me the best of personal and professional support: Julia Balaisis, Bob Barton, Jim Giles, Christine Jackson, Sandra Katz, Steve Lieberman, Peter Mansell, Jeanie Nishimura, Debbie Nyman, and Pat Quigley
- Mother, for the love
- David Booth, for the mirrors and windows

An Overview

DRAMATHEME	GAMES	DRAMA EXPLORATION	SOURCE	ASSESSMENT PROFILE
Humor	Joining In	Choral Dramatization	Nursery Rhymes	Choral Dramatization
Mystery	Communication	Questioning/Interviewing	*The Mysteries of Harris Burdick* (picture book)	Communication
Fantasy	Imagination	Theatre Crafts	"The Grebigol" (story)	Group Participation
Animals	Physical Activity	Movement	*The Music of Dolphins* (novel)	Physical Activity
Relationships	Cooperation	Character	*I Met a Bully on the Hill* (script)	Participation
Folklore	Personal Narrative	Storytelling	Traditional Tales	Storytelling
Community	Trust	Role Playing	Map	Role Playing
The Past	Concentration	Writing in Role	Photographs	Writing in Role
The Future	Negotiation	Problem Solving	*The Giver* (novel)	Problem Solving
Diversity and Equity	Problem Solving	Interpretation	*Skin* (script)	Interpretation

About This Book

"Drama teachers must have the opportunity to redo, rerun, or improve a lesson. Just as we always afford the students the possibility of slowing down the work, rehearsing or changing their minds, so too must we be as flexible with ourselves."

Kathleen Gallagher,
Drama Education in the Lives of Girls: Imagining Possibilities
(2000, p. 116)

Dramathemes was written with the intention of giving teachers a travelling companion as they embark on drama journeys in their classrooms. Since it was first published, many teachers across the country have been appreciative of the practical ideas and structures that this guide has offered them. They have ranged from those teachers who were only beginning to use drama and who sought strategies for introducing their students to the world of "Let's pretend" to those who were much more familiar with the structures provided in *Dramathemes* and who shaped their own work around them. I thank you all.

This newly revised third edition has been written to provide you with an updated version of games, activities, and resources on the ten themes that framed the original two books. I have attempted to weave together favorites from the first two editions and have revised the descriptions and framework to make the book more accessible to meet current curriculum initiatives. The foundation of this resource remains the same, since I have held the belief that literature can be the focus and springboard of drama explorations and that themes provide a "hook" for the teacher in making connections to story and to fellow class members. In this book, I have included a variety of literary genres, such as nursery rhyme, picture book, poetry, fable, novel, and script, not only as a means of suggesting ideas for activities, but also to engage the imagination and to enrich the creativity and thoughts of our students.

The ten chapters of this book are based on popular thematic explorations in literature for young people:

- Humor
- Mystery
- Fantasy
- Animals
- Relationships

- Folklore
- Community
- The Past
- The Future
- Diversity and Equity

The pages that follow describe some of my own experiences working in classrooms in the Peel Board of Education during the past twenty-five years, as well as with the hundreds of children I met in the past decade in my role as drama consultant. It is my contention that these "dramathemes" can be used with all grade levels. Each group of students is unique, and it is the students who create the action. Your beliefs, experiences, training, and level of confidence as a teacher will determine the starting points, paths, and ends that you and your students will encounter on your journey. You are invited to select and modify ideas within the units to support your curriculum needs, your language program, and the interests and needs of your students.

To help you choose appropriate strategies, the chapters in *The New Dramathemes* have been structured in this way:

Introduction
- an overview of the chapter's theme
- a listing of learning opportunities

Games
- activities, games, and exercises organized by skill focus and introducing concepts explored in the theme

Drama Exploration
- verbal and non-verbal activities to stimulate imagination and communication, promote physical and social growth, and develop role-playing and improvisation skills

A Drama Structure
- an exploration of a literary source
- a scheme outlining a variety of conventions to structure drama over a period of time

Beyond the Drama
- extensions of the theme through writing, reading, art, and drama activities

Assessment Strategies
- observation guides, each with a focus area of language, social, and drama learning
- self-assessment profiles to help students reflect on their learning

Recommended Sources
- an updated list of literature on the theme, including picture books, poetry anthologies, novels, non-fiction, and scripts

In this new edition you will find a variety of sources for storytelling, improvisation, interpretation, and movement; guides for planning drama; novel response activities; reproducible blackline masters of sources, assessment profiles, and activities; drama conventions with descriptions; and rubrics for evaluation.

No book can serve as a definitive statement on practising drama. The updated list of titles in References (pages 158–59) will provide you with support, as they have given to me. In particular, much gratitude goes to Jonothan Neelands and Tony Goode for the book *Structuring Drama Work* and for providing a rich menu of drama conventions and a significant framework for structuring our work. This resource and others will help you find answers to your questions about teaching drama. That said, the answers to your questions won't be found only on the pages of books. The discovery and the learning for both you and your students will happen as you live through imagined experiences in your classroom.

1/Humor

As teachers, we want our lessons to stay in children's heads and hearts, to guide their decision-making and problem solving in later life.

Alistair Martin-Smith, "The Explosive Imagination,"
in *Writing in Role* (1998, p. 97)

• •

Source: Nursery Rhymes

TEACHER: What would you ask Humpty Dumpty if he came into the classroom?

STUDENT: Who pushed you?

Theme Overview: *No teacher's manual or curriculum guide tells us if Humpty Dumpty was pushed, what happened to him after he fell, who he spoke to, or why he was sitting on the wall. In this dramatheme, the strange situations in which rhyme characters find themselves invite students into the world of humorous situations where their imaginations can take charge.*

Learning Opportunities
- To participate in getting-acquainted games that develop a sense of belonging to a group
- To practise the skills of interpretation and experiment with pitch, pause, and pace to read rhymes aloud chorally
- To familiarize students with the rhythms, patterns, and themes of a variety of nursery rhymes
- To contribute ideas to a choral presentation and to support the contribution of others
- To unravel meanings of a short text by raising questions, hypothesizing, role-playing, and improvising
- To explore the stories within the stories of playground and nursery rhymes

• •

Games: Focus on Joining In

Introductions
Students stand in a circle. One person begins the game by saying his or her name and performing an action or gesture, such as clapping hands above the head, wiggling, or bending over. The group echoes the name and the movement. The game continues until each person has become the leader who calls out his or her name.

EXTENSIONS

- The names are called out in a dramatic way (e.g., a shout, a cheer, or a whisper), and a new gesture is provided to accompany the name. Encourage students not to repeat any actions that have already been presented.
- This time each group member repeats the action from the previous activity, but does not call out any name. The mimed gesture may help group members remember participants' names.

Greetings
1. On a signal, students walk around the room introducing themselves to one another, shaking hands.
2. On another signal, students resume walking around the room and greet one another, touching toes. The game continues with partners connecting with different parts of the body (e.g., elbows, ears, knees).
3. Students create greetings that might be used by aliens on a strange planet. They walk around the room and introduce themselves using their new greetings.

EXTENSION

- Students form a circle which represents a council meeting of alien creatures. One student demonstrates his or her greeting, and the group echoes the movement presented. The activity continues around the circle until every person has demonstrated a greeting. An alternative is to have only a new sound greeting presented.

What's in Your Name?
In this game, students work in a variety of group situations as they seek others whose first names share a characteristic with their first names. As students circulate, tell them to find others whose names

- start with the same initial as theirs
- share at least two of the letters in their names
- have the same number of vowels that their names contain
- have the same number of letters that their names contain
- have the same number of syllables that their names contain

EXTENSION

- Have students work with their last names.

Name Scrabble

This game can be played by giving the students small Post-it notes, one for each letter of their name. For example, a student named Chris would get five Post-it notes and write each of the letters in his name on a note (C H R I S).

Students unscramble letters in their first names to make as many words as possible. As an example, a student named Deborah could derive the words *bed*, *dear*, *are*, and *had* from her name. When students have exhausted all possibilities, they team up with a partner. Combining letters from both names, they make as many words as possible.

EXTENSIONS

- Students work in groups of four to make words using only the letters from their first names.
- Students use their first and last names to play the game.

Thinking about Our Names

Provide the following questions to students to prompt discussion or to use as a questionnaire when interviewing one another.

- Do any words rhyme with your name?
- Without unscrambling any letters, what words can you find in your first name? in your last name?
- How many words can you make when you unscramble the letters of your first name?
- Who were you named after?
- Do you have a middle name?
- Do you know your name in another language?
- Do you have a nickname?
- What is the name of a pet that you know? How did the pet get its name?
- Do you like your name?
- What name would you choose for yourself?
- If the vowels in your name were given one point and the consonants two points, what would the score for your name be?

Human Bingo

Human Bingo is a suitable get-acquainted activity (see page 12). It is also appropriate to use when members of a class need to integrate with one another in a non-threatening way.

Each player has his or her own copy of the bingo sheet. The point of the game is to try to find a player who matches the information in a square. When players find someone who matches the information in a square, they ask him or her to sign it. The first player to fill a horizontal, vertical, or diagonal line calls out "Bingo."

The game can continue by making the task more difficult. For example, perhaps the player must fill in a specified line, four corners, two diagonal lines, or the entire sheet in order to win.

At the end of the game, students share information that they've learned about their classmates.

Human Bingo

Has the same birthday month as you	Has at least one initial the same as you	Wears glasses	Owns a cottage	Has been to Florida
Is not wearing running shoes	First name has the same number of letters	Can say hello in three languages	Has two brothers	Is wearing an earring
Has freckles	Has a cat	**X**	Likes liver	Has blue eyes
Is wearing a belt	Prefers vanilla to chocolate	Has an allergy	Can play a musical instrument	Has a dog
Can do ten pushups	Is wearing something red	Likes doing crossword puzzles	Is smiling	Knows a nursery rhyme

Drama Exploration: Focus on Choral Dramatization

Chanting Our Names

Students practise chanting their names aloud in a variety of ways, for example, in a whisper, mysteriously, musically, as if being surprised, as if meeting a long-lost friend, or as if being called by robot.

Acting Out Alliterative Adjectives

Students think of an alliterative adjective to describe themselves (e.g., *Sly Sally*, *Dynamic David*, *Amiable Amanda*). On a signal, they walk around the room and introduce themselves (e.g., *"Hello, I'm Dynamic David"*) to as many people as they can in one minute. The activity is then repeated with the students acting in a manner that reflects their alliterative adjective. As an extension, students could add an alliterative verb (e.g., *Dynamic David digs*) and mime the activity as they meet people.

Dancing Our Names

Using the total number of syllables in their first and last names, students clap a rhyme to accompany their names. As an extension, they could create a movement or gesture to accompany each syllable of their name. Students then work in pairs to create a dance or movement that expresses both partners' names. This activity can be extended to a group of four.

Tongue Twisters

A fun way for students to practise read-aloud skills is to repeat tongue twisters (see page 14). Each twister should be repeated three times, going from slow to fast. Students can challenge one another to see who can say one of the tongue twisters most often.

- shining soldiers
- a proper copper coffee pot
- three free throws
- six seasick sheep
- This is a zither. Is this a zither?
- Sugar sacks should be shaken.

Here are some longer tongue twisters to practise. Before working on them independently, students can attempt to read them in unison, or echo individual words or lines as you call them out.

Sheep shouldn't sleep in a shack. Sheep should sleep in a shed.

If Stu chews shoes, should Stu choose the shoes he chews?

I saw Esau kissing Kate,
And Kate saw I saw Esau,
And Esau saw that I saw Kate,
And Kate saw I saw Esau saw.

A tooter who tooted a flute
Tried to tutor two tutors to toot.
Said the two to the tutor,
"Is it harder to toot or
To tutor two tutors to toot?"

Tongue Twisters

- toy boat

- coal oil

- unique New York

- red rubber, blue blubber

- black bug's blood

- sixty-six sick chicks

- a big blue bucket of blue blueberries

- a sure sign of sunshine

- Glowing goblins gleam.

- Plump pumpkins play.

- Is Ruth's tooth loose?

- Brenda blew big blue bubbles.

- Trudy chewed two chewy cherries.

- Nat's knapsack strap snapped.

- Which silk shoes did Sue choose?

- Blair bumped Burt. Burt burped.

I thought a thought. But the thought I thought wasn't the thought I thought I thought. If the thought I thought I thought had been the thought I thought, I wouldn't have thought so much.

Swan swam over the sea
Swim, swan, swim;
Swan swam back again,
Well swum, swan.

A fly and a flea
Flew up the flue,
Said the fly to the flea,
"What shall we do?"
"Let's fly," said the flea.
"Let's flee," said the fly.
So they flew up a flaw
In the flue.

Finger and Clapping Rhymes

Many students are familiar with playground or nursery rhymes, such as "Miss Mary Mack Mack Mack," "Doctor Knickerbocker," "See, See My Playmate," "A Sailor Went to Sea Sea Sea," and "Eensy-Weensy Spider." They say or sing these rhymes aloud with friends, often accompanying the rhymes with actions or clapping rhythms.

i) In this activity, students teach partners action rhymes, adding finger and hand actions, such as clapping hands, snapping fingers, slapping knees, or clapping a rhythm. Students repeat the rhyme, increasing their speed each time or saying the rhyme in various ways, for example, whispering, then shouting.

Two little bluebirds
Sitting on a hill.
One named Jack.
One named Jill.

Fly away, Jack.
Fly away, Jill.
Come back, Jack.
Come back, Jill.
Two little bluebirds
Sitting on a hill.

Onery, Twoery,
Ziccary can.
Hollow bone, crack-a-bone,
Ninery ten.

Spit spot,
It must be done.
Twiddlum, twaddlum,
Twenty one.

Here are Grandma's glasses.
And here is Grandma's hat.
And here's the way she folds her hands
And puts them on her lap.

Here are Grandpa's glasses.
And here is Grandpa's hat.
And here's the way he folds his arms
And takes a little nap.

My boyfriend gave me apples.
My boyfriend gave me pears.
My boyfriend gave me fifty cents
And kissed me on the stairs.

I gave him back his apples.
I gave him back his pears.
I gave him back his fifty cents
And kicked him down the stairs.

Here are some additional humorous rhymes to chant.

I never saw a purple cow,
  I hope I never see one;
But I can tell you anyhow,
  I'd rather see than be one.

There was an old woman
  Lived under a hill;
And if she's not gone,
  She lives there still.

Lucy Locket lost her pocket;
  Kitty Fisher found it.
Not a penny was there in it,
  Only ribbon round it.

Cock-a-doodle-doo!
  My lady has lost her shoe,
And master's lost his fiddling stick.
  Sing cock-a-doodle doo.

Hoddley, poddley,
  Puddles and frogs,
Cats are to marry
  Poodle dogs.
Cats in blue jackets.
  And dogs in red hats,
What will become of
  The mice and the rats?

ii) There are more than ten body parts that students can point to as they say this next rhyme aloud.

Chester, have you heard about Harry?
He just came back from the army.
Everyone knows that he tickles his toes.
Hip, hip, hurray for the army!

iii) Students accompany the chant below with appropriate actions. They might suggest other paired items or instructions that could be sung aloud, too.

Head and Shoulders, Baby, One Two Three!
Head and Shoulders, Baby, One Two Three!
Head and Shoulders, Baby, One Two Three!
Head and Shoulders, Head and Shoulders,
Head and Shoulders, Baby, One Two Three!
(patty-cake clap)
... Knees and Ankles, Baby, One Two Three!
... Ears and Eyebrows, Baby, One Two Three!
... Throw the Ball, Baby, One Two Three!
... Milk the Cow, Baby, One Two Three!
etc.

Rhymes Aloud

Drama Convention: Choral Dramatization

Choral dramatization invites students to read aloud such texts as rhymes and poems by assigning parts among group members. By working with peers to read aloud poems on a particular theme or topic or by a single poet, students take part in a creative activity that involves experimentation with voice, sound, gesture, and movement. Because of these variations, no two oral interpretations of a single poem are alike.

Choral dramatization enhances students' skills of reading aloud and presentation. More important, however, when students work in small groups to read aloud together, their problem-solving skills are likely to be enriched as they make decisions about the best way to present a poem.

A familiar poem, such as "This Little Piggy," easily allows students to experience choral dramatization techniques described in "Ten Ways to Read a Rhyme Out Loud." Once the students have practised several ways to say the words aloud, they can decide upon some actions to accompany each line.

This Little Piggy went to market.
This Little Piggy went home.
This Little Piggy had roast beef.

This Little Piggy had none.
And this Little Piggy cried, "Wee wee wee"
all the way home.

Note: If you divide the class into five groups, each group can invent a story about what happened to a piggy.

Planning Guide
Ten Ways to Read a Rhyme Out Loud

1. **Echo reading:** The teacher says one part; the students repeat what the teacher says.
2. **Alternate reading:** The teacher says one line; the students say the next line.
3. **Unison:** Once the students are familiar with the rhyme, they can say the poem aloud together at the same time. The teacher can join in as a member of the group.
4. **Cloze technique:** In this technique, at least one word is omitted. The students can join in and say those words. Leaving off the last word in the line is a simple cloze technique.
5. **Two groups:** The class is divided into two groups. Each group can read the lines alternatively. Repeating a reading of a selection with each group reversing parts works well.
6. **Assignment of lines:** The class can be divided into groups, with each group assigned a line of the selection or a verse of a longer selection. Also, individual students could be assigned a line, a part of a line, or a word to contribute to the shared reading of the poem.
7. **Use of soft and loud voices:** The words of the selection can be said in a whisper or in loud voices. Or, the lines can be said gradually going from soft to loud or from loud to soft. Similarly, students can say the poem slowly to quickly.
8. **Rhythm clapping:** As students say the lines, they clap along with the rhythm of the selection (or tap knees, or snap fingers). They can also clap hands with a partner as they say a poem aloud.
9. **Singing:** Sometimes, rhymes can be sung to familiar tunes. For instance, "Humpty Dumpty" could be sung to the tune of *Happy Birthday to You.*
10. **As a round:** The class is divided into two groups. Group One begins to read the selection and continues until the end. Group Two begins the selection after Group One has begun. Both groups finish saying the poem at a different time. Once familiar with the technique, the class can be divided into three or more groups to present a round.

Time to Share Rhyme

It is most appropriate to introduce this activity after the students have explored a variety of ways to read a poem aloud in a shared reading experience with the whole class. Students work in pairs or groups of three, and

Rhymes about Pigs

To market, to market, to buy a fat pig.
    Home again, home again, jiggety-jig.
To market, to market, to buy a fat hog.
    Home again, home again, jiggety-jog.

Tom, Tom, the piper's son
Stole a pig and away he run.
The pig thought it was quite a treat
To be carried down the street.

Upon my word and honor,
    As I went to Bonner,
I met a pig
    Without a wig
Upon my word of honor.

There was a little pig
Who wasn't very big,
So they put him in great big show.
While playing in the band,
He broke his little hand,
And now he can't play his old banjo.

Higglety, pigglety, pop!
The dog has eaten the mop;
    The pig's in a hurry,
    The cat's in a flurry,
Higglety, pigglety, pop!

Dickery, dickery, dare!
The pig flew up in the air;
    The man in brown,
    Soon brought him down.
Dickery, dickery, dare!

each group is given a nursery rhyme to read aloud chorally, for example, any of the rhymes on page 18. Once the choral reading has been practised, each small group could share its rhyme with another.

Note: You could assign two groups the same rhyme. When they present their rhymes to each other, they can compare their different interpretations.

A Drama Structure: Flying-Man

The following drama structure encourages students to look inside and outside a piece of text. Because they are short, because there is a possibility of uncovering other stories within the story, and because a problem or dilemma is suggested, rhymes are particularly effective for developing a drama unit. In *Telling Stories Your Way*, storyteller Bob Barton observes:

> For the past forty years I have never lost my fascination for nursery rhymes. Above all else I have enjoyed using these powerful elliptical stories with students and extending them into exciting narratives.
>
> As a result, the work of taking a minimal text and building on it I value highly. I think this activity is tremendously important for helping students to see the possibilities of taking the germ of an idea and elaborating on it. (p. 109)

Planning Guide
A Scheme for Using Rhymes

Strategy	Function
Game	to build interest; to set the context
Choral speaking	to experience the text
Discussing	to interpret and speculate
Questioning	to build commitment; to explore puzzles
Interviewing	to explore events; to build roles
Storytelling	to develop narrative
Meeting	to negotiate meaning; to problem-solve
Reflecting	to investigate possibilities; to hypothesize
Extending	to explore the moment/the past/the future

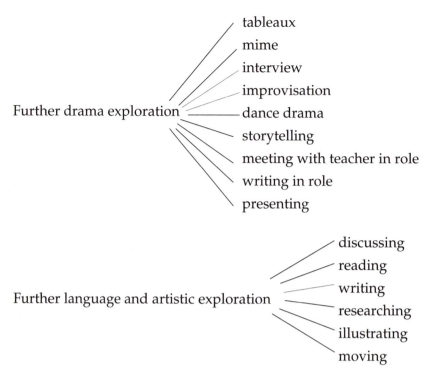

Further drama exploration
- tableaux
- mime
- interview
- improvisation
- dance drama
- storytelling
- meeting with teacher in role
- writing in role
- presenting

Further language and artistic exploration
- discussing
- reading
- writing
- researching
- illustrating
- moving

For Bob Barton, the simple challenge offered for story and drama exploration is to ask these three questions:

- Who is speaking the words?
- To whom is the speaker speaking?
- Why is the speaker saying this?

Some familiar rhymes, such as "Humpty Dumpty," "Little Miss Muffet," "This Little Piggy," or "Old Mother Hubbard," provide stimuli for developing character and inventing plots. Some question-and-answer poems are also appropriate sources, since they provide appropriate contexts for interviews, for example, "Pussycat, Pussycat/Where Have You Been?" and "Mary, Mary, quite contrary/How does your garden grow?"

The following structure, based on "A Scheme for Using Rhymes," outlines my experiences using a rhyme, "Flying-Man," with a primary class. Following the framework outlined, I provided students with an opportunity to raise questions, dig for stories, and accept the invitation to fly.

Flying-Man

Flying-Man, Flying-Man,
Up in the sky,
Where are you going
Flying so high?

Over the mountains
And over the sea.
Flying-Man, Flying-Man,
Can you take me?

Game: Students worked with a partner. One student became the "clay," while the second student took on the role of sculptor. Sculptors were instructed to create statues of nursery rhyme, fairy tale, or story characters with which they were familiar. Without speaking, they shaped the clay to create poses. Once sculptors finished their work, their partners tried to guess who they were. The activity was then repeated, with sculptors and clay switching roles.

Choral Speaking: As a group, we chanted the rhyme, "Flying-Man." Students experimented by saying the rhyme in a variety of ways, including soft to loud voices, call and response, as a round, clapping, and singing (to the tunes of *On Top of Old Smokey* or *Twinkle, Twinkle, Little Star*).

Individual students were given a single word from the rhyme and the poem was read aloud. The activity was then repeated, with each student saying the word as dramatically as possible. Students concluded the activity by chanting their line, adding a movement, and then freezing into a position.

Discussing: Students discussed the facts that they knew from reading the lines of the rhyme. They were also eager to offer their predictions of who the flying man might be and what adventure he might have had.

Questioning: I posed the following scenario to the students: "If Flying-Man was to come into this room, what questions would you like to ask him?" Students informally talked about questions with classmates before sharing them in a whole-class discussion. I listed the following questions on chart paper:

How is he able to fly?
How far will he go?
Is he meeting someone?
Will he take someone with him?
How will he choose other people who can go with him?
Where does the man live?
Who saw him fly?
Can the flying man hear the person?
How long can he stay up in the sky?
What can the flying man see from the sky?

Interviewing: I asked the students to think about who, besides Flying-Man, would be able to answer these questions. They suggested possible characters that could be used in the drama: the flying man's best friend, a farmer, his wife, his children, a bird, the stars. Some children volunteered to assume these roles. In turn, different characters, in role, sat before the class to answer questions. The scene was set for them in the following way:

You have all seen or heard about Flying-Man. Many of you have travelled far to find out if the flying man will take you with him. In a few moments, you will be able to find out from others who have seen or known Flying-Man. In this meeting, you will have a chance to find out from others any information that is known about the flying man.

Note: Alternative Ways of Interviewing
- The teacher works in role as Flying-Man or as someone who saw Flying-Man.
- The students work in groups of three. One person witnessed the man flying; the others, as reporters or visitors, investigate the story.
- Volunteers are chosen to assume roles of people who know something about Flying-Man. They are placed about the room, and students wander over to them to learn more about the story.

Storytelling: The students, in small groups, played villagers who had been chosen to accompany Flying-Man on his trip. They created a story about their adventure, describing where they went, what they saw, any problems they had, and why the event was so special. They could decide if it was a humorous, magical, or frightening adventure. The villagers were asked to reflect on the adventure and recall it years later to others who might wish to go on the trip. To share their stories, new groups were formed.

Meeting: The students met as relatives of Flying-Man. Flying-Man flew so high that when he reached the moon, he decided not to return home. The relatives were concerned about his safety, but also wanted to convince the man about all that he would miss on Earth. The teacher, in role as Flying-Man, listened to arguments that would try to persuade him to return home.

Reflecting — Illustration: The students were invited to illustrate a scene that depicts a flying adventure as a memory to share with others.

Extending — Writing: Students reflected on their work in the drama by completing one of these activities:

- Add another verse(s) to continue the rhyme, using the question-and-answer format of the original.
- Make a request/invitation to Flying-Man via a letter.
- Write a story that explains how Flying-Man got his power to fly.
- Prepare a newspaper article covering the event of a man flying in the sky.
- Compose a diary entry that Flying-Man might have written.

Extending — Drama: Students could discuss the similarities between "Flying-Man" and the following nursery rhyme:

> There was an old woman tossed up in a basket
> Nineteen times as high as the moon;
> Where she was going, I couldn't but ask it,
> For in her hand she carried a broom.
>
> "Old Woman, Old Woman, Old Woman," said I,
> "O wither, O wither, O wither, so high?"
> "To brush the cobwebs off the sky!
> And I'll be back again by and by."

Taking the two rhymes together, students could pursue these explorations:

- Interviewing: What questions might Flying-Man ask the old woman?

Rhyme Extension

Flying-Man, Flying-Man
Flying around,
Why are you flying
So far from the ground?

Flying-Man, Flying-Man
Flying so slow,
Flying-Man, Flying-Man
Where will you go?

- Storytelling: What stories did the neighbors tell about these flying people?
- Designing: What kinds of flying devices might others use to fly high in the sky?
- Movement: Retell the story of a flying adventure in movement only.

Beyond the Drama

Miming a Rhyme
Students work independently to create a mime story of a familiar rhyme. Once they have done so, they perform it for a partner who tries to guess the rhyme. Students may need to be reminded to slow their actions to help make their mime presentations clear. Each partner should have a turn at guessing a rhyme.

Creating a Class Anthology
The class creates an illustrated anthology of recess or nursery rhymes with each student in the class illustrating one rhyme. Students can choose the medium — cut paper, markers, crayons, tissue paper, whatever. They can also determine whether illustrations will appear together or on separate pages.

Classifying Rhymes
Many anthologies present rhymes in sections or chapters according to a theme or characteristic. Using their class collection, students categorize their rhymes into sections. In groups of four or five, students take a copy of the poems and classify them in any way they wish, for example, by number of lines, by animal characters, or by gender. You might limit students to three categories for classification.

Finding Rhyme and Pattern Books
Students create classroom collections of other rhyme and pattern books under one of these categories:

- alphabet books
- nursery rhyme collections
- counting books
- lullabies

- song books
- joke and riddle books
- rhymed stories

Working in groups to gather books for one category, students create an annotated bibliography. Group members choose their favorite book from each category and share it with the rest of the class.

Interviewing a Nursery Rhyme Character
Students choose which nursery rhyme character they would like to be. Working in pairs, they can conduct an interview between a nursery rhyme character and a magazine reporter. Each student should have a chance to tell a story from a character's point of view.

Extension: These stories could be written as magazine articles. Younger students might paint pictures representing magazine photographs. They could write captions to accompany the photos.

Continuing a Rhyme

Students, in small groups, record a rhyme on a large sheet of paper. Invite them to write one or more stanzas of this nursery rhyme, continuing the story from the first stanza. They should use the same rhyme scheme, patterning their poem on the original one. Once each group has prepared a rhyme, they can present it chorally. These choral readings could be shared as a class or tape-recorded for other classes to hear.

Making a Mother Goose Museum

The class decides as a group what items they would like to include in a museum built for Mother Goose. Items in the museum might include drawings, posters, puppets, costumes, props, tape recordings, a mural story, hats, written stories, food, Plasticine models, scenery designs, magazine photographs, and dioramas.

The students can work individually, in pairs, or in small groups to prepare the Mother Goose Museum. On a Mother Goose afternoon, another class could come to see the museum. What will the students wear to it? What food might be served?

Recommended Sources

Beaton, C. 2001. *Playtime Rhymes for Little People*. New York, NY: Barefoot Books.

Beck, I. 1988. *Little Miss Muffet*. Oxford, UK: Oxford University Press.

Booth, D. 1993. *Doctor Knickerbocker and Other Rhymes*. Toronto, ON: Kids Can Press.

Brown, M. 1987. *Play Rhymes*. New York, NY: E. P. Dutton.

Denton, K. M. 1998. *Nursery Rhymes*. Toronto, ON: Douglas & McIntyre.

Dunn, S. 1999. *All Together Now*. Markham, ON: Pembroke Publishers.

Graham, C. 1979. *Jazz Chants for Children*. New York, NY: Oxford University Press.

Hoberman, M. A., and M. Emberley. 2001. *You Read to Me, I'll Read to You: Very Short Stories to Read Together*. New York, NY: Little, Brown.

Hoberman, M. A., and N. B. Westcott. 2000. *The Eensy-Weensy Spider*. New York, NY: Little, Brown.

Hort, L., and G. B. Karas. 2000. *The Seals on the Bus*. New York, NY: Henry Holt.

Lee, D., and D. McPhail. 2000. *Bubblegum Delicious*. Toronto, ON: Key Porter Books.

Martin, D., and S. Meddaugh. 1998. *Five Little Piggies*. Cambridge, MA: Candlewick Press.

Opie, I., and R. Wells. 1999. *Here Comes Mother Goose*. Cambridge, MA: Candlewick Press. (Also: *My Very First Mother Goose*)

Polacco, P. 1995. *Babushka's Mother Goose*. New York, NY: Philomel Books.

Sabuda, R. 1999. *The Movable Mother Goose*. New York, NY: Simon & Schuster.

Sierra, J., and J. E. Davis. 2001. *Monster Goose*. San Diego, CA: Harcourt, Inc.

Swartz, L., D. Booth, J. Booth, and L. Booth. 2001. *Out Loud: Rhythms, Rhymes and Chants for Language Learning*. Toronto, ON: Lingo Media.

Assessment: Focus on Choral Dramatization

Name: _____   Date: _____

	Always	Sometimes	Never
Does the student …			
use voice appropriately to convey mood and intent?	❏	❏	❏
recognize his or her role in the ensemble?	❏	❏	❏
contribute ideas to the choral presentation?	❏	❏	❏
support the contributions of others?	❏	❏	❏
have an appropriate sense of audience?	❏	❏	❏
follow directions and accept advice?	❏	❏	❏
experiment with pitch, pause, and pace to make the reading more effective?	❏	❏	❏
investigate a variety of possibilities for using voice, sound, and movement?	❏	❏	❏
understand the significance of revising/rehearsing?	❏	❏	❏
seem committed to the task?	❏	❏	❏

Comments:

_____

_____

_____

_____

_____

2/Mystery

True drama for discovery is not about ends; it is about journeys and not knowing how the journeys may end.

Dorothy Heathcote, in Dorothy Heathcote: Collected Writings on Education and Drama (1984, p. 98)

Those of us who are interested in education recognize the significance of questioning as the means by which teachers help students to construct meaning. We also know that the collective construction of action which gives voices to that meaning is dependent upon the students' skills in asking productive questions.

Norah Morgan and Juliana Saxton, Asking Better Questions (1991, p. ix)

· ·

Source: *The Mysteries of Harris Burdick*, a picture book by Chris Van Allsburg

Theme Overview: *Mystery stories and poems let us journey into places and problems that are not part of our real lives. Solving a mystery is like following an old treasure map — you have to add all the clues and details to come up with a suitable solution or perhaps continue on a path of puzzles where other treasures or detours might be discovered. In this dramatheme, students become drama detectives caught in a mystery web woven with question marks and imagined stories.*

Learning Opportunities
- To practise communication skills through games and activities
- To take and use effectively the opportunities within the drama that require speaking and listening
- To develop questioning skills, both in and out of role
- To conduct interviews by taking on a role
- To participate as experts by working in role as those who know
- To extend investigation, enquiring with imagination and exploring novel ideas appropriate to the theme
- To accept and build on the ideas of others
- To interpret and create a response to both stimulus material (illustration) and the teacher in role

· ·

Games: Focus on Communication

Word Association

This popular word game invites players to voice spontaneous thoughts that arise in response to words spoken by another player. Encourage players to make associations freely and tell them that they needn't explain their word associations. The game begins by having one player saying a word, such as "book," "water," or "tree." The second player responds to that word by saying the first word that comes to mind. The first player then responds to that word. The play continues until one or both players decide to end the game.

EXTENSIONS

- The game is played in groups of four.
- Players clap a rhythm (e.g., three claps) between each player's turn.
- Players respond with words that have no association to the last word spoken (e.g., water, bench).
- Players write their answers, later shaping the words into a poem or script; pairs can exchange their work to read aloud.

Drawing Directions

This game provides students with an opportunity to demonstrate effective oral communication skills by giving and following directions accurately. To begin, students find a partner and sit back to back.

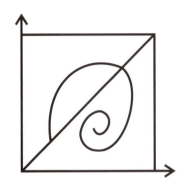

With paper and pencil, one student begins by drawing a simple picture, such as the one shown at left. The student then gives directions that will allow the partner to duplicate the picture. To make the activity easier, listeners may be allowed to question their partners. To make the activity more difficult, instructions for more intricate designs can be given, or a rule that no questions may be asked can be set. At the end of the game, partners compare their creations with the original designs.

EXTENSION

- Students make up their own designs and *write* accurate directions for others to follow, rather than give oral instructions.

Pictionary

The class is divided into groups of four or five. Each group is given a large sheet of paper and a few markers of any color. The members of the groups are numbered off (1, 2, 3, 4).

The teacher gathers all the 1's together and tells them a word that they are going to draw, for example, *lamp, jewellery, surgery, magic, story,* or *garden.* Each word could be written on a card. 1's rush back to their groups and, on a signal, begin to communicate the word by drawing quickly on the paper. The first group to guess the word correctly wins. Scores can be kept. The game is repeated until each member has had a chance to draw at least once.

The game could be repeated by using

- themed words (*storm, sunshine, blizzard, hurricane, weather*)

- book titles (*The Lion, the Witch and the Wardrobe; The Bible; The Wizard of Oz; Pippi Longstocking; Where the Wild Things Are; The Secret Garden*)
- proverbs (A stitch in time saves nine; You scratch my back, I'll scratch yours; Behind every cloud is a silver lining)
- historical figures (George Washington; Cleopatra; Noah; William Shakespeare)

EXTENSION

- Repeat the game, this time as a relay. 1's are the first to draw pictures. As soon as a group guesses the word, 2 goes to the teacher to get a new word for the group to guess, and as soon as the group has guessed, 3 receives a word to play. The first team finished wins.

Sixes

Students sit in a large circle. One player is chosen to sit in the centre with his or her eyes closed. On a given signal, an object (e.g., ball, ruler, pen) is passed around the circle from neighbor to neighbor. At any time, the player in the centre claps his or her hands, making the player who has the object "It." The player in the centre calls out a letter of the alphabet. "It" must name six objects that begin with that letter within the time it takes for the object to be passed to him or her again. (If the circle is small, the object can be passed around two times.) If "It" is successful, the game continues with the object being passed until the player in the centre claps hands again. If the new "It" cannot name six objects beginning with that letter, she or he replaces the player in the centre.

EXTENSION

- Players in the centre could specify criteria: for example, each word must have two syllables or fit a category (e.g., cities, animals, foods).

A Bag/A Rag

Once the students catch on to this game, it tends to be a favorite. To begin, the game is played in groups of eight to ten students. Eventually, the whole class plays it. One person, perhaps the teacher, is Player One. This role demands some concentration, and the person in this part is responsible for keeping the game going. The following script best demonstrates how the game is played:

> PLAYER ONE (to Player Two): I give you a bag.
> PLAYER TWO (to Player One): A what?
> PLAYER ONE (to Player Two): A bag.
> PLAYER TWO (to Player Three): I give you a bag.
> PLAYER THREE (to Player Two): A what?
> PLAYER TWO (to Player One): A what?
> PLAYER ONE (to Player Two): A bag.
> PLAYER TWO (to Player Three): A bag.
> PLAYER THREE (to Player Four): I give you a bag ...

Once the game is under way, Player One turns to the player on his or her left, saying, "I give you a rag." The rag segment is passed around the circle simultaneously with the bag. At some point, a player will get the bag and the rag — the trick is to pass both on, in either direction.

EXTENSION

- Other rhyming word pairs can be used to play this game, for example, cat/hat, hen/pen, bone/stone. Sometimes, players pass an object in either direction as they say their lines. Doing this may simplify the game — or perhaps cause more confusion!

The Magical Pencil

Students sit in a circle of five or six. In their possession is a magical pencil that can be transformed into anything they'd like it to be. For instance, the first person might use it as though brushing teeth, and the second person might use it as a flashlight. After each person has performed an activity that demonstrates what the pencil has become, he or she passes it to the person on the right. The game continues for as long as the students seem to be interested. If a person can't think of an activity, he or she can say "pass"; however, when the pencil arrives back, he or she should be ready to mime. Encourage students not to speak during the activity. Most of the group may confirm that they understand what the person has done by nodding their heads. If the group members seem confused, then the person should repeat the activity, more slowly or with more mime. After ten minutes or so, the group can discuss some of the unusual things that the pencil became.

Variations: Instead of a pencil, students could use a roll of masking tape, a scarf, or a piece of rope.

Drama Exploration:
Focus on Questioning and Interviewing

Witness

Students work in pairs or in small groups. One person is chosen to be the storyteller/witness; other players are to be the lawyers. The lawyers are free to interrupt the storyteller at any time and to ask for details that will add to the story being told.

> WITNESS: One day last winter ...
> LAWYER: What day was it?
> WITNESS: It was a Tuesday.
> LAWYER: What was the temperature that day?
> WITNESS: It was windy and chilly.

EXTENSIONS

- Students take turns so that everyone has the chance to role-play both the storyteller and a lawyer.
- Group sizes may change so that there can be more than one lawyer or witnesses in the interview.

What's the Question?

Like the television show, *Jeopardy*, this activity invites students to think of questions that relate to words and phrases. As an example, "school" might prompt such questions as "Where do you go every morning?" "Where do you learn things?" and "What do you call a group of fish?" Students can work in pairs or groups of three to brainstorm questions for the following words and phrases:

- in the basement
- in the newspaper
- Jamaica
- beside the police station
- blue

- It's too cold
- my aunt
- money
- zero
- Never!

EXTENSIONS

- Students, individually, in pairs, or in small groups, write at least three questions that correspond to each word or phrase. (If there is time, they provide questions for all.) Once they have completed their lists, they join other students to compare questions.
- With a partner, students choose three questions that they think are most dramatic. They improvise a conversation between two characters, using one of the questions as an opener. Students decide beforehand who might be speaking and why they might be having this conversation.
- As an alternative activity, students work with a partner to conduct a conversation in which both participants can only ask questions. The challenge is to maintain the conversation as long as possible without the use of a statement.

Gathering Evidence

1. Students work in groups of four, with each group given a large envelope. Members fill the envelope with eight to twelve objects from their pockets, knapsacks, or desks. When prompted, they imagine that these objects all belong to the same person and that they have been gathered as evidence against that person by the police. As a group, students use the objects to build a story around this character.
2. After each group has worked out the background of their character, they pass their envelope to another group. Two of the members move with the objects, and two remain behind so that new groups of four are formed.
3. On a signal, the police (the two original partners) reveal their evidence to the private investigators (the two new partners). The private investigators try to determine the story behind the evidence. The police should be prepared to answer questions, but do not have to tell the investigators everything they know.
4. Students return to their original groups and develop or revise their stories based on the investigators' questions and explanations.

- Students conduct a whole-class improvisation where each detective group uses its evidence to present a case. Students, as investigators, try to connect the stories.
- Students continue the investigation by calling witnesses to testify.

The Question

Explain to the class that you are going to begin a drama just by asking a question. The question that you ask should explain who a character is, who the students might be, and what the problem is.

Here are sample questions that can be used to begin the improvisation:

- Are you sure you don't want to join me on my Ark?
- Why isn't that pyramid finished yet?
- Do you have proof that there is life on other planets?
- What can we do about all these rats in our village?
- Does anyone know when the knights will be returning?
- When did you first notice the trouble in the boat?
- How are we ever going to impress the king?
- Are we going to stay in our homes under these conditions?
- Don't you agree that we should build the railroad?
- Who here is brave enough to let the General know how we feel?

Once the drama begins, invite students to ask questions or give any information that they feel might contribute to the improvisation. Allow the session to continue for as long as the students seem interested. After the improvisation, you might ask the students to report who they were, where they thought they were, and how they might continue the drama.

The Dark, Dark Bottle

Read aloud or make copies available of the poem "A Dark, Dark Tale." After listening to or reading this traditional story, the students can pretend that they are holding the bottle that was found in the dark, dark house. You, as curator of the local museum, have come to interview the students about the bottle, which has not yet been opened. Some sample questions:

A Dark, Dark Tale

On a *dark, dark* street
there was a *dark, dark* house.

In the *dark, dark* house
there was a *dark, dark* room.

In the *dark, dark* room
there was a *dark, dark* cupboard.

In the *dark, dark* cupboard
there was a *dark, dark* shelf.

On the *dark, dark* shelf
there was a *dark, dark* bottle.

And in the *dark, dark* bottle
there was a …

- What color is the bottle?
- What's so unique about it?
- How is it opened? (a cap? a cork?)
- Are there any special markings?
- Do you think the bottle is worth a lot of money? Why?
- Is it in good condition?

- Do you think someone left the bottle there on purpose?
- Where do you think it came from?
- Are there any sounds or smells?
- Are you nervous about owning the bottle? Why?
- What do you think you'll do with the bottle?

As a follow-up, have the students, in pairs, discuss what they think should be done with the bottle.

Once again in the role of the museum curator, announce that a small "Do Not Open" label has been found on the bottle. Let students discuss whether they think the bottle should be opened or not.

- Students can draw what they think emerges from the bottle.
- Students can work in small groups to build a story about the bottle's past, which they can report at another meeting.

A Drama Structure: *The Mysteries of Harris Burdick* by Chris Van Allsburg

On the flyleaf to this popular picture book by Chris Van Allsburg, it says, "For those who have thought themselves as unimaginative, this book will prove the opposite. Even the most reluctant imagination, when confronted by these drawings, will not be able to resist solving the mysteries of Harris Burdick." The titles of the pictures, the lead sentences, the surreal drawings, and the premise of the disappearing author make this a rich source for drama. The book prompts students to raise questions and work in role to build stories, to make hypotheses, and to solve a problem.

The following sample (page 33), entitled *The Third-Floor Bedroom*, is accompanied by the line "It all began when someone left the window open." Who is that someone? How is this room connected to Harris Burdick? What adventure began with the opening of the window? The answers lie inside the head — and inside the drama!

Hiring Detectives: The lesson began with the teacher asking the class to consider why someone would need the help of a detective.

After brainstorming on this topic, the teacher explained that the drama was going to involve a group of detectives trying to solve a mystery. The teacher invited the students to work in pairs to conduct interviews for hiring detectives. One partner had a turn at applying for a detective's position with the government. The interview was then repeated by having the students switch roles. Each interviewer was instructed to find out about the candidate's training, employment record, disguises, expertise, family background, special talents, any significant case(s), possible ownership of an agency, dangers that the detective had faced, and so on.

Drama Convention: The Mantle of the Expert

When students wear "the mantle of the expert," characters in the drama have a special knowledge that is relevant to a situation or task. The mantle of the expert empowers the students and provides them with responsibility, information, and respect. For more about this topic, see *Drama for Learning: Dorothy Heathcote's Mantle of the Expert Approach* (1995) by Dorothy Heathcote and Gavin Bolton.

After the interviews, the teacher brought all the detectives together and explained that because they'd all be working together for a while, it would be necessary for each detective to report an interesting piece of personal background experience that would describe the qualities he or she would bring to the job.

The Third-Floor Bedroom

It all began when someone left the window open.

The Case Begins: The teacher introduced himself as the Chief of Police. He had been given to understand that the students were all competent detectives and welcomed them to this emergency session. He explained that help was needed and that they had been called in to assist him in solving a rather baffling case. The teacher announced:

> It seems that a man named Harris Burdick disappeared quite some time ago. His family is quite concerned about the bizarre case. Apparently Harris's life was rather peaceful and he never seemed to have any enemies. The only information that headquarters has is a photograph that was sent to Police Headquarters. This photograph is under tight security at the moment, but I hope to be able to share it with you at our next meeting. I realize you have many questions and I will try to provide some answers. I'm afraid, however, that the information we have is rather limited, which is why we're depending on your expertise.

The session continued with the group questioning the teacher closely and listening carefully to the answers that were given. In response to their questioning, it emerged that Burdick was a photographer who had won many prizes; he was a quiet family man; his family was on vacation at the time of his disappearance; he had held many jobs in the past; and he had been alone in the house.

Drama Convention: Questioning

Questions are used by the teacher both inside and outside drama explorations, both in role and out of role, to give purpose, direction, and shape to the learning activities. Questions can stimulate the minds of students and help them go beyond what they already know. When teachers and students ask questions, they can be drawn into fictional contexts and awakened to universal themes and concepts of the drama rather than just the storyline. Questioning can deepen belief and commitment and help students to reflect on the work and on their personal views. When working in role, the teacher can use questions to challenge simplistic solutions, move the action along, or slow it down to promote deeper consideration of the characters, tensions, and issues being explored.

The following chart offers an analysis of Dorothy Heathcote's question modes as David Booth worked with a group of Grade 1 students exploring the story *The King's Fountain* by Lloyd Alexander. The playmaking experience was videotaped, and in this session the students worked through the problem of dealing with a king who has taken away their water. Booth assumed the role of the king, and the students, as villagers, were challenged to determine their fate.

DOROTHY HEATHCOTE'S QUESTION MODES	EXAMPLES	STUDENT RESPONSE
Seek information	• What did you find out (from the king)?	• You're taking the water/ He'll wash his crown.
	• What are you going to do about it?	• We'll hide the water.
	• Where will you get the water from?	• From the king's fountain.
	• Why are you taking the water?	• We want to drink it.
	• I don't know what to do now.	• You should give half to him and half for you.
	• He puts two of your friends in jail. He won't let you take the water. What is your next plan?	• Disguise yourself as the king.
	• What kind of clothes would a king wear?	• Gold clothes/a gold tongue
Assess interest	• Will you tell that to the king when he comes?	• Yes.
	• Who thinks they are going to be disguised as a king?	• (volunteers)
	• How could you fool the guard?	• Have two kings.
Supply information	• What does it say on your shield?	• Fight/Fight the villagers.
	• What else did you use the water for?	• The water makes every-thing grow.
	• What will he wear when he is disguised as a king?	• a beard/his crown/his clothes
Branch: To decide on a course of action	• Why don't you use your own water instead of my fountain?	• You took it.
	• Should we make him a king or him a king?	• Him, because he'll give us water.
	• Will you come with me, or will you stay in the vil-lage?	• I'll stay with you because you're the best king.
Control	• I'm taking (your) water from the river. Right, guards?	• Right!
	• Now, I'm not the king. Is that clear?	• (Nod heads)
	• Do you think you can do it?	• Yes.

DOROTHY HEATHCOTE'S QUESTION MODES	EXAMPLES	STUDENT RESPONSE
Establish moods and feelings	• Won't there be guards on duty? • Did I just hear something? What could it be? • Guards, are you ready?	• We'll shoot a rock in his face. • It must be one of the villagers sneaking up./Two maybe. • Yes.
Establish belief	• What kinds of weapons do you have? • My guards, are you ready? • It seems that he is taking everything away from you. Is this true? • Will you rule fairly?	• I have a spear. • Yes. • Yes. • Yes.
Deepen insights	• What is the problem if I take away the water? • What will you do when the buckets of water are gone? • Do you think I should build a new fountain?	• We'll all die. • We'll get the water back. • Two fountains — so they will check the wrong one.

* See *Drama as a Learning Medium* by Betty Jane Wagner (1976/1999, p. 61).

In a chapter entitled "The King and I," which appears in his 1994 book, *Story Drama*, Booth describes his work with this story during the past three decades and shares his goals for drama:

> I want drama to deepen the children's understanding of themselves and others, and where they live, as they build an improvised world through a process of group interaction. Although I encourage them to create imaginary gardens, their response to the problems, conflicts and characters must be real. How the teacher elicits both commitment and authenticity is what is important to true learning. (p. 58)

These goals and question modes hold true for work with *The Mysteries of Harris Burdick*.

The Detectives Prepare: The teacher brought the students out of their roles and, as a group, they discussed all the facts that were learned about Harris Burdick. Students also had an opportunity to share their predictions and hypotheses about Burdick's story. The teacher then asked the students to work in small groups with their fellow "detectives." On large sheets of paper, they prepared questions that they would like to have answered. The session concluded with the teacher acting in role and receiving the questions from the various groups. These questions were recorded on a large sheet of paper for future investigation.

Sample Questions
- How was the photograph sent to headquarters?
- Has there been any contact with Burdick's family?
- Is there a possibility that this is a publicity stunt?
- What other jobs has Burdick had in the past?
- What prizes has he won?
- Is his life in danger?
- Did he have any enemies?
- Could Harris Burdick have sent the picture to the detectives?

Introducing Evidence: The teacher, in the role of the Chief of Police, thanked the detectives for their inquiry and work to date. He explained that some of the detectives might be wondering why they were chosen for the case. The drama was set up by offering the following:

> The files indicate that somewhere in the past each of the detectives may have been involved with a situation involving Harris Burdick or someone who knew him. Though it is a common name, these people might be able to bring some insight into the man's past and perhaps give some clues about his disappearance. If you are able to share some of the information with your colleagues, we might be able to gain further insight into the mystery. Also, you might have some information about this picture which up until now was kept private [picture was taken from a sealed envelope].

The students, as detectives, examined the photograph and offered further speculations about its role in Burdick's story.

A few detectives reported past cases that explained some episodes from Burdick's life and contributed background information. The Chief of Police thanked the detectives for this information and said that he felt they were ready to investigate. The Chief explained that he realized they might have more questions and perhaps a few minutes could be taken to discuss these. The students, as detectives, worked in small groups, brainstorming a list of further questions they'd like answered.

Interviewing Witnesses: The teacher, out of role, asked the class to provide a list of characters they might like to speak to in order to get some information about Harris Burdick (his wife, his partner at work, a next-door neighbor, his son, his publisher, his father.) The teacher invited six students to volunteer, each to take one of the roles. The six students were not given a chance to discuss their roles/stories amongst themselves, but, one by one, they were questioned by the group of detectives. Each interviewer spoke for about two minutes, and each was briefly interrogated by the teacher in role as the Chief of Police.

The detectives were then given an opportunity to wander about the room and interview one or more of the six characters to clarify any details and to further build Burdick's story, perhaps making corrections between the various stories revealed. The session concluded with the detectives working together in groups of four or five to share their information and build a story that would be presented at the next meeting.

Digging into the Past: The students collected objects, magazine photos, or pieces of writing that might tell the story of the past and/or disappearance of Harris Burdick. The teacher conducted a meeting of all the friends, family, neighbors, acquaintances, and fellow workers that Burdick might have known. Students in role explained who they were, how they knew Burdick, and what pictures or objects or pieces of writing they had that would reveal Burdick's life story.

> ### Drama Convention: Objects of Character
>
> This convention helps students to flesh out a character by assembling a variety of objects or personal belongings that serve as clues about the owner. These items can be "discovered" as a way of introducing a character to the drama. Once the group meets this person in role, the behavior may confirm or contradict the group's interpretation.

The Mystery Is Solved?: The teacher explained that in order to piece together Burdick's story, groups could create scenes from the man's life that would explain his disappearance. These scenes were to be presented as a series of tableaux (three or four). Each tableau would represent a picture that could be further used as a clue to Harris Burdick's disappearance. The students were given some time to prepare their tableaux stories.

At another meeting of detectives, each group shared its work, presenting further "picture" clues as evidence. After doing so, the students discussed any needed corrections between the stories and together built a single Harris Burdick story. A final discussion was held to find out whether the students felt all their original questions were solved and if there were any other questions that they felt could be answered.

Beyond the Drama

Making Mystery Pictures

Students could create their own mystery pictures that might illustrate a scene that would explain Burdick's disappearance. They could give titles and captions to their pictures. These illustrations could be drawn from the tableau scenes presented in the drama. Students could use markers or pencils or perhaps white drawing pencils on black construction paper to create a photographic effect.

Writing Detective Reports

After the drama, students could write a detailed report to the Chief of Police describing what they know about Burdick's disappearance.

Writing the Stories Behind the Pictures

In the introduction to the book, Chris Van Allsburg claims that, before he disappeared, Harris Burdick had written many stories to accompany the pictures, "some hilarious, some frightening, some bizarre." The students are told to imagine that they are Harris Burdick and are invited to write the stories that might have accompanied the pictures that Burdick might have given to his book publisher.

Making More Mystery Stories

One or more pictures from *The Mysteries of Harris Burdick*, by Chris Van Allsburg, can be used for further storytelling. The class could be divided into small groups with each group creating a story about what happened before the scene in the picture, during the scene, and after the scene. Each group could decide how to tell the story behind the picture (e.g., in tableaux, in movement, through improvisation, by Story Theatre, through illustration, through writing).

Extension: Once each group has shared its story, the class discusses these questions:

- Are there any connections amongst any of these pictures?
- What details in any of the pictures might give clues to Burdick's disappearance?
- Does the sequence of the pictures have any significance?

Designing a Set

The students work in groups to create a room for Harris Burdick. Using furniture, pictures, objects, and articles of clothing, they can create a space for the detectives to investigate and discover clues about Burdick. They can think of designing a set for a play version of Harris Burdick's life. They might choose to create another room in the house where the story began or perhaps a room that Harris Burdick disappeared to.

Drama Convention: Creating an Environment

Students use available material and furniture to define a space where a drama is happening as accurately as possible. A room, a garden, a factory, a jail cell, and a restaurant are examples of sets that can be designed to physically represent where events have taken place or are talked about in the drama.

Recommended Sources

Brown, R. 1991. *A Dark, Dark Tale.* New York, NY: Scholastic Inc.

Clarke, G. (ed.). 1996. *The Whispering Room: Haunted Poems.* New York, NY: Kingfisher.

Myers, C. 2000. *Wings.* New York, NY: Scholastic Inc.

Nilson, A. 2000. *Art Fraud Detective.* New York, NY: Kingfisher.

Van Allsburg, C. 1983/1996. *The Mysteries of Harris Burdick.* Boston, MA: Houghton Mifflin. (Also available in *Portfolio Edition*)

Van Allsburg, C. 1986. *The Stranger.* Boston, MA: Houghton Mifflin.

Wynne-Jones, T., and I. Wallace. 1988. *Architect of the Moon.* Toronto, ON: Douglas & McIntyre.

Assessment: Focus on Communication Skills

Name: _____   Date: _____

Does the student …	Always	Sometimes	Never
reveal thoughts willingly?	❐	❐	❐
explain and describe ideas clearly?	❐	❐	❐
take turns during discussions?	❐	❐	❐
accept and build on the ideas of others?	❐	❐	❐
make positive suggestions to complete tasks and build the drama?	❐	❐	❐
raise significant questions?	❐	❐	❐
conduct interviews effectively?	❐	❐	❐
communicate thought in role?	❐	❐	❐

Comments:

_____

_____

_____

_____

3/Fantasy

I too require passion in the classroom. I need the intense preoccupation of a group of children and teachers inventing new worlds as they learn to know each other's dreams. To invent is to come alive. Even more than the unexamined classroom, I resist the uninvented classroom.

Vivian Gussin Paley, *The Girl with the Brown Crayon* (1997, p. 50)

Everyone is an artist. Whoever creates is an artist; and who does not create?

Hughes Mearns, *Creative Power* (1929, p. 152)

. . . .

Source: "The Grebigol," a story

Theme Overview: *The drama journey takes us to places both real and imagined to meet people both real and imagined. By creating fictional contexts, we can explore life around the corner, in other kingdoms, or on other planets. In this dramatheme, the private world of fantasy can be shared with others as the students encounter a strange creature in their imaginations — and in their classroom.*

Learning Opportunities
- To express imaginative ideas when contributing to the drama work development
- To contribute effectively in group and pair work, enhancing self-esteem and that of others
- To brainstorm and reflect on several solutions to a problem
- To speak in role as characters in a story, using the vocabulary and portraying the attitudes of those characters
- To create masks, illustrations, and writing that can be used within the drama experience
- To self-assess contributions to small-group activities

. . . .

Games: Focus on Imagination

Creativity Inc.

Students work in pairs or in small groups to complete this creative thinking activity. Invite them to imagine that they work for a company called Creativity Inc. Their job at the company is to develop lists of ideas to help others think creatively. Ask them to brainstorm solutions to one of the following problems within a time limit of three minutes. Groups can compare lists to discover which ideas are original.

- List things that are soft.
- How many ways can you use a rope?
- How would you entertain a crying baby?
- Name foods that have double letters.
- What jobs will there be in the future that do not exist today?
- Name things that have holes.

- How many ways can you win something?
- How many words can you make from the word "dinosaur"?
- What are some ways to recycle a plastic cup?
- Invent new ice-cream flavors.
- Why does the world need numbers?
- Why does the world need books?

EXTENSIONS

- Repeat the activity, assigning a new topic for the students to brainstorm. Students first work individually, then in pairs, then with a group of four to compare lists.
- In groups, students work to solve a different task. Challenge each group to brainstorm the longest list of items for their company.

What's the Use?

Challenge students to name as many ways as possible that the items below can be utilized. As an example, a button could be used as an earring, the eye of a teddy bear, a surfboard for a tadpole, and a placemat for wet spoons. Also, remind students that in brainstorming all responses are accepted and tell them that they should be prepared to explain their answers. To prepare the students for brainstorming, they might work together as a whole group to record ways that a plastic cup may be used. Each pair or small group could then be assigned the same item or a different item from the list.

- an umbrella
- a bead
- a chair
- a sock

- a candle
- a suitcase
- a roll of masking tape
- an empty bottle

Paired Drawings

Students work in pairs to demonstrate non-verbal communication and to examine interaction and cooperation. Each pair is given a large sheet of paper and one crayon. Ask them to hold the crayon together so that both can draw at the same time. On a signal, students are asked to create a picture, but are not allowed to speak. Both students proceed to draw until they have finished a picture to their mutual satisfaction. After the activity, students discuss how they felt about it. How did the two partners communicate? Did they cooperate? Was there a leader? How satisfied are they with the picture?

Note: To help students, some music might be played as they draw their pictures, or students might create a drawing in response to a poem or story.

EXTENSIONS

- You could allow the partners to speak, have students find a new partner and not speak, or assign a specific picture to be drawn.

Invention Convention

1. Students become expert inventors and create a *watchyamacallit* out of any material or materials they wish. The *watchyamacallit* that they create will be the one item that they think is missing from this world. The poem that follows should prompt some ideas.

   A Watchyamacallit

   Is there a watchyamacallit inside your head?
   Is it small and blue or big and red?
   Can you use it on Tuesdays to brush your hair?
   Can you use it to sit on instead of a chair?

   Did you see someone use one while painting a wall?
   Was it made from an eraser or a rubber ball?
   Is the watchyamacallit something heavy or light?
   Is it used to make our world turn bright?

   Is it a contraption to catch a wee mouse?
   Or an elephant scrubber as big as a house?
   Make your invention from any junk that you find.
   A watchyamacallit grows and grows in your mind.

   L. S.

2. Students then work in small groups where they imagine that they are all expert inventors. They are going to meet fellow inventors at an Invention Convention, where they will share creations with one another. Each person could explain to fellow inventors how the *watchyamacallit* works and why it would be useful to the world. They could also describe how they decided upon this invention. The students should be prepared to answer any questions that these expert inventors might have about their products.

EXTENSION

- Students could create a *watchyamacallit* museum in the classroom, displaying all their inventions. Descriptions and instructions should accompany each invention.

Tell Me What to Draw

Students work in pairs with a piece of paper and a pencil or marker. Players sit back to back or far apart from one another so that they don't see each other's paper. Partners take turns giving instructions about a detail that could be added to create a drawing of an alien. After each instruction, both partners draw what has been requested. Each player should have a chance to provide six to eight instructions. At the activity's conclusion, students compare their drawings to determine their success at giving and following instructions.

PLAYER 1: Draw a large circle.
PLAYER 2: In the middle of the circle, make a nose the shape of a banana.
PLAYER 1: Add two eyes that are shaped like hearts.
PLAYER 2: Put a polka-dot hat on its head.

If I Could Be ...

This activity helps students to think about who they are, what they would like to be, and what they want to do. The following statements could be written on the board or on a worksheet. Students fill in their answers privately before sharing them with others.

If I could be an animal, I'd be a(n) _____ because _____.
If I could be a color, I'd be _____ because _____.
If I could be a famous person, I'd be _____ because _____.
If I could be a number, I'd be _____ because _____.
If I could be a letter of the alphabet, I'd be _____ because _____.
If I could be a song, I'd be _____ because _____.
If I could be a food, I'd be a(n) _____ because _____.
If I could be a piece of furniture, I'd be a(n) _____ because _____.
If I could be a musical instrument, I'd be a(n) _____ because _____.
If I could be a shape, I'd be _____ because _____.
If I could be a flower, I'd be a(n) _____ because _____.

Other possibilities include car, building, tree, word, candy, country, insect, dessert, season, body of water, and flavor.

Note: With younger students, it's best to give a choice. For example: "Would you rather be a robin, an elephant, or a cat?" "Would you rather be an ocean, a river, or a lake?"

Would You Rather ...?

Each student is given a copy of "Would You Rather ...?" (page 45). Ask students to fill in each item by circling one choice. Once all of them have completed the sheet, the students wander about the room to get autographs for each of the items. An autograph is given if two students have the same item. To encourage interaction, tell students that they can ask a person only one question when pairs meet. If both items match, then they can sign each other's sheet. If someone answers that they already have a signature for that item, then he or she may ask another question. The object of the game is to get twelve different signatures.

Would You Rather …?

1. Would you rather be the color …

   a) blue
   b) green
   c) yellow
   d) red

2. Would you rather eat …

   a) fish and chips
   b) a hamburger
   c) steak
   d) spaghetti

3. Would you rather own …

   a) a hamster
   b) a tarantula
   c) a rabbit
   d) a snake

4. Would you rather visit …

   a) Paris
   b) the North Pole
   c) Egypt
   d) Australia

5. Would you rather play …

   a) a game of cards
   b) checkers
   c) the guitar
   d) the radio

6. Would you rather …

   a) fly to the moon
   b) dig for treasure under the sea
   c) explore a haunted house
   d) discover a castle

7. Would you rather be …

   a) a painting
   b) a song
   c) a sculpture
   d) a poem

8. Would you rather buy …

   a) a book
   b) a CD
   c) a box of chocolates
   d) flowers

9. Would you rather be the letter …

   a) A
   b) S
   c) Q
   d) G

10. Would you rather be …

   a) a king
   b) a genie
   c) an invisible person
   d) a giant

11. Would you rather be …

   a) a bird
   b) a fish
   c) a lizard
   d) a tiger

12. Would you rather talk to …

   a) Curious George
   b) Cinderella
   c) Humpty Dumpty
   d) The Wizard of Oz

- Survey the items to find which are most popular.
- Students may form groups based on having more than five things in common. In their groups, they decide which place in 6 they would prefer to travel to. They could create three pictures (tableaux) that show what happened on their adventure.

Drama Exploration: Focus on Theatre Crafts

Creations

Here is an exercise in creativity, as well as non-verbal communication. The teacher should prepare beforehand an envelope or a box containing a variety of materials, such as scissors, construction paper, straws, tape, paper clips, elastics, wool, newspaper, tinfoil, cardboard strip, and glitter. Each kit could be the same, or each kit could have different materials. To launch the exploration, the teacher reads aloud "The Grebigol" or makes copies of the blackline master available to the students (see next page).

1. The class is divided into groups of three or four, the students sit in a circle at a table or on the floor, and a kit is given to each group.
2. Tell the class that each group is going to work together to produce a single Grebigol creature, using any of the materials from the kit. Alternatively, they could create a dragon, a bird, a forest or sea creature, or an alien being.

   Explain to the class that, until the activity is completed, *no one may talk.* Students may neither speak nor pass notes to one another. Allow 15–25 minutes.
3. Once the creatures have been completed, put them on display for the other groups to view.
4. After the creatures have been seen, each group should discuss how it felt to assemble their creation, especially without talking. The self-assessment profile on page 56 could be used at this time.

EXTENSION

Students work in small groups to create a four- to six-line rhyming poem to accompany the creations. Poems, which can be written on small file cards, can be used to tell someone a small story about the creature.

Once groups have written the poems, they could prepare a choral reading. Members decide how each line could be read, how parts could be divided, what sounds could be added, and what movements or formations could be used to present the poem.

Sample Poem

His tail is strong and hairy.
His teeth are green and scary.
The creature comes from far away.
Will he leave tonight or will he stay?

The Grebigol

Winter has left its mark upon the land. The hills and valleys are empty, desolate and stark. Nothing moves. The trees are blue and black against the frozen earth. Everything is waiting for spring.

Slowly, slowly, as the earth tilts back upon its axis, warmth is coming to the icy world. The snow is beginning to melt away, the rivers are catching the snow as it melts and begins its journey to the sea. Fresh, tender grass is beginning to break through into the sunlight ... the forest is beginning to come to life.

Somewhere high in those mountains is a long forgotten valley — a peaceful and beautiful valley. The earth stirs and begins to rumble. Is it an earthquake? The chipmunks stop dead in their tracks. The birds cease their singing. The earth buckles up, cracks and crumbles and begins to fall away. Something is coming up out of the earth, out of the depths of the den where he has slept away the long cold winter. It is the giant GREBIGOL.

The GREBIGOL is hungry. He hasn't eaten all winter. He begins to eat the new fresh grass. He reaches down and gobbles down new saplings, berries and bushes. He is devouring the chipmunks, the birds and the foxes. As he eats, he is heading down the canyon.

As he nears the town, he begins to eat telephone poles. He eats a dog and a cat. He swallows two garbage cans, a gas station and a policeman. Now he is eating a new Volkswagen. He eats everything in sight ... eating, crunching, munching and gobbling until finally he is satisfied. Full. He cannot eat any more.

His eyelids are getting heavy. He is stuffed and getting very tired. Slowly, painfully, he begins to pull himself back up into the mountains, back to his den where he will dig his way back down into the earth. He will sleep there for another year until he is hungry again!

Author unknown

Mask Design 1

The following format could easily facilitate the making of masks for students to build stories with or use in their dance dramas or rituals.

Provide each student with a photocopy of the face on page 49. They should make masks somewhat larger than their own faces and may decorate the masks in any way, for example, by creating geometric or abstract designs. They may also use markers or colored pencils. The masks can be worn by attaching tongue depressors which the students can hold (see diagram 2) or by attaching cardboard strips worn on the head (see diagram 3).

EXTENSIONS

- The students are told that their designs must be symmetrical.
- The students use only black-and-white construction paper to decorate their masks. The designs can be quite powerful for presentation.
- The students create sun masks, using only the colors red, orange, and yellow (see diagram 4).

Mask Design 2

Students can make creature masks using paper bags, paper plates, papier-mâché, or other materials. One easy method that allows for a variety of possibilities is outlined below.

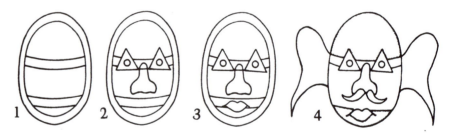

Needed materials include bristol board strips, about 3 cm (1 inch) wide for each student: 1 long strip, 2 short strips; scissors; assorted construction paper; glue and/or staples; and miscellaneous materials, such as yarn, foil, tissue paper, crepe paper, stickers, glitter, ribbons.

Staple the two ends of the long strip and then the two shorter strips onto that frame (see diagram 1). The students may decorate their masks in any way, by attaching eyes, a nose, a mouth, ears, antennae, horns, a moustache, whatever. They should be encouraged to make their shapes as *large* as possible, filling in as much area as possible, still leaving a space enabling them to see. Strings or elastic should be attached to the mask so it

Mask Design

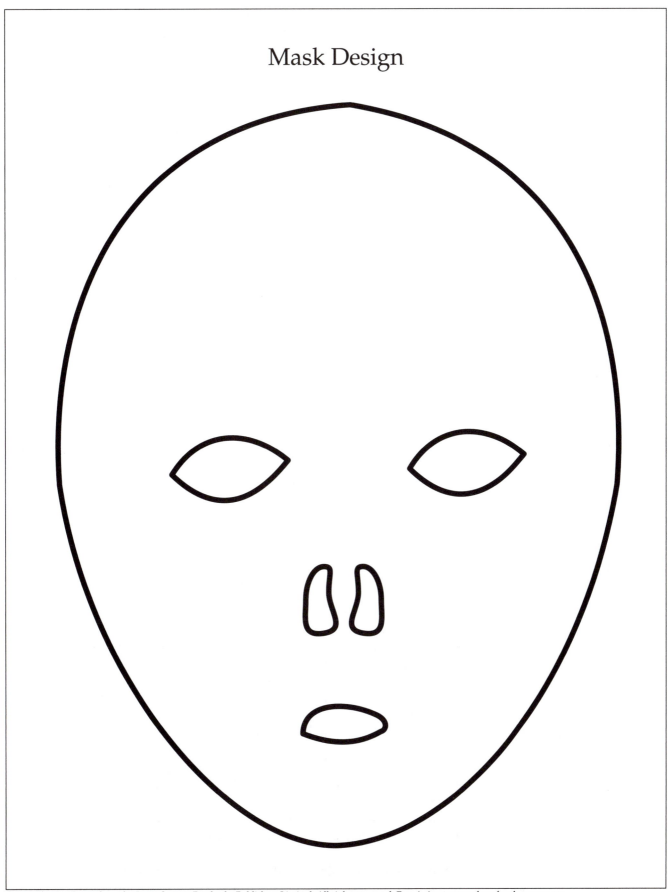

can be worn. Students wear the masks to become the creatures and move about as these creatures might, perhaps making sounds.

EXTENSIONS

- Working in small groups, each student tells a story about the creature behind his or her mask.
- Students perform mirror exercises, using masks in pairs or in small or large circles.
- Students create a large group tableau of alien creatures invading another planet. They should come to life very, very slowly. On a signal, they could freeze into various positions, and on another signal come to life again. Repeat this a few times. Alternatively, the students could come to life cumulatively, with one person beginning to move, then another and then another until the whole class comes to life as masked creatures.

A Drama Structure: "The Grebigol"

Teachers are often faced with the dilemma of structuring a drama unit when they are allocated only short blocks of time, for example, forty minutes, to work with the students.

The timetable at left outlines my experiences with a unit on creatures. Lessons that explored a different drama focus for each day are outlined below.

Episode One: The Creature Approaches
Use the rhyming couplet from *The Judge* by Harve and Margot Zemach:

> A horrible thing is coming this way,
> Creeping closer day by day.

Here are some suggested ways of chanting the lines:

- The whole class reads lines together.
- The teacher calls out lines; the class responds.
- The class is divided into two groups (boys/girls; left side/right side; front/back). Group 1 calls out the first line; Group 2 responds (and reverse).
- The class says the lines repeatedly from loud to very soft, from soft to loud, from slow to fast.
- The class claps a rhythm to accompany the lines.
- Group 1 shouts the first line; Group 2 responds, saying the second line in a whisper.
- Each word is assigned to a different student.
- The lines are sung, perhaps in operatic or country and western style.
- The lines are said in very spooky or frightened voices.
- The lines are broken up: *A horrible thing/Is coming this way/Creeping closer/ day by day.*
- Students stand when they read aloud their lines.
- Different students read the first line solo, and the class responds with the second line.
- Students say the lines as if they're the ... funniest ... saddest ... most serious ... silliest lines they've heard.

Planning Guide

Timetable for a Drama Unit

Day 1	• Choral dramatization • Brainstorming • Interviewing witnesses
Day 2	• Meeting and planning • Making Wanted posters
Day 3	• The Creature's Story • Still images
Day 4	• Problem solving • Meeting to report
Day 5	• Movement • Writing in role

Sample Couplets

It talks through its nose.
It has slimy toes.

or

His mouth breathes smoke.
He wears a green cloak.

Extension: The students could work in pairs to create a rhyming couplet that would describe the horrible thing that's coming this way.

Each pair should decide how to present its couplet, by dividing the lines or the words, with movement and/or sounds. Each pair, in turn, presents its couplet to the rest of the group.

Brainstorming: Students, sitting in a circle, were invited to become members of a village who are convinced that some alien creature is approaching them. They held a village meeting at which each student, in turn, described one thing that he or she knew about the horrible thing coming their way (e.g., It is mauve; it has feathers; it has silver antennae). The game continued around the circle several times. This brainstorming activity encouraged the students to go beyond physical description and to discuss the creature's background, personality, likes and dislikes, hobbies, interests, etc.

Interviewing Witnesses: The students, working in pairs, were given the following instructions:

A's: *You are members of the village* who have seen the horrible thing coming your way. You can describe the creature fully: you can give information on what it did, what it ate, where it came from, and what trouble (if any) it has caused.
B's: *You are media reporters* from the newspapers, television, or radio who have been told to get the story about the horrible thing. Your questions should help you gather important information so that the world can learn about this creature.

See "Paired Improvisations Were Successful: Now What?" (page 52) for further ideas.

Extension: After the first interview, partners could reverse roles and repeat the improvisation. With the creature getting closer, the witnesses could provide more detailed information about its behavior.

Episode Two: Making a Plan

A Meeting: A meeting of media reporters is held to discuss the horrible thing that is on its way. Questions, such as these, arose: What do we know about the creature? What should newspaper headlines or news bulletins say? What should we be concerned about? The teacher, in role as one of the village citizens, answered the questions. Other students volunteered to tell stories as other witnesses to the creature's actions.

Wanted Posters: Using the information presented in the improvisation, students created a Wanted poster depicting the image of the monster. Accompanying the poster, students wrote a physical description of the creature and explained why it was wanted.

Variation: As newspaper reporters, students prepared a newspaper article describing the creature and telling the story of its appearance. A headline and drawing (representing a front page photo) accompanied the article.

Planning Guide
Paired Improvisations Were Successful: Now What?

The following outline details strategies to be employed after paired improvisations, such as those described previously. These strategies are particularly useful if students are working in the context of media reports.

1. Reporters stand. They report what they heard to the teacher in role as interviewer.
2. Storytellers stand. They report their story to the teacher in role as interviewer.
3. Storytellers stand. They find a new partner to whom they tell their story. The new partner becomes the interviewer.
4. Storytellers, reporters, or both conduct a meeting to share stories, for example, a press conference, an editorial meeting, or a city council meeting.
5. Storytellers and reporters form partners. They create a tableau image that encapsulates a story that was told. They could create two additional tableaux to show what happened before and what might happen next, as well.
6. Partners enact the improvisation while audience members watch to learn new information about a character.
7. Partners switch roles and repeat the improvisation.
8. Partners switch tasks. The interview is conducted in some "future" time.
9. A third person is added as a witness who reports what was discussed *or* is given a role to contribute to the interview.
10. The information provided in the interview is used as a context for writing in role. Students might write a letter, a report, or a diary entry.

Episode Three: The Creature's Story
Students met in groups to develop a background story. Who, if anyone, sent the creature here? Where did the creature come from? Why is it here? What does it want to do here? see here? How did it arrive here?

Once they decided upon the story, the students worked to present it in a series of three to five still images, or tableaux. Each image represented one part of the creature's story. They then met with another group to share their work. Students discussed the messages and stories behind each group's presentation.

Episode Four: What's to Be Done?
The students, in role as witnesses to the creature, arranged a meeting to discuss what should be done. They expressed concern about the damage that was caused already and the potential danger of keeping the creature here. The students were told that the creature's life must be preserved. If killed, other creatures might take revenge. At the meeting, suggestions were offered. In order to deal with the creature appropriately, it was

Drama Convention: Still Image

Working alone, with a partner, or in small groups, s[...] still image using their bodies to crystallize a moment [...] drama. By creating a frozen picture with others [...] required to discuss, negotiate, and make a decision up[...] will communicate or represent their ideas.

Still images can be shared by one group watching another, or, the large group can be an audience as the work is presented. As these images, or tableaux, are interpreted, students should be encouraged to brainstorm many messages that may be contained within a single image.

To enrich still image work, students need to consider the following:

- *Multi-levels:* Are students arranged in high, medium, and low positions?
- *Balance:* Is the arrangement between figures balanced?
- *Focus:* What is the scene's focus of attention? Where will the viewers' eyes rest?
- *Body Language:* What feelings and meanings will be conveyed through gestures and facial expressions?

When more than one tableau is created to depict a story or theme, students need to consider transitions from one image to the next. Cues from the teacher (e.g., snapping fingers, clapping, banging a tambourine, counting, or the accompaniment of music) could encourage this.

Note: An alternative way of creating a still image is to have individuals act as sculptors to shape an image.

decided that it would need to be caught and put in an environment that would do it no harm.

Students met in small groups to devise a plan to present to the authorities about the creature. A large sheet of paper was given to each group.

Once a plan for capturing the creature was completed, each group sent a representative to the mayor (teacher in role) to present their ideas.

Beyond the Drama

Creating Creatures
First, students move independently.

- On a signal, the students freeze into positions that represent creatures.
- On another signal, they make a sound that they think their monsters or creatures might make.
- They are then instructed to move very slowly about the room as monsters or creatures. They may also make sounds and greet other creatures they meet.

Students could also create monsters in pairs or in small groups.

Extension: The teacher calls out activities that the creature can do; the students do these activities, each in their own spaces. Examples include turning heads in many directions, eating something, drinking, dancing, greeting another creature, riding a bicycle, getting dressed, and playing tennis. Musical accompaniment that suggests how the creature might move enhances this activity.

Making Group Monsters

The students stand in a circle and number themselves. Person 1 is instructed to go into the centre of the circle and create part of a creature. On a signal, 2 enters the middle of the circle and adds on to the creature. The class continues until the whole group is part of the creature.

Extension 1:   The teacher calls out numbers at random or taps students on the shoulders to prompt creation of a new monster. Each student could make a creature sound that should be repeated until the whole monster has been created. Likewise, the sounds could diminish, one by one, by having the teacher call out numbers once again and by having each student stop making his or her sound when the number is called.

Extension 2:   Instead of the teacher calling out numbers, students spontaneously add on to the monster as they wish.

Alien Conversations

The students, working in small groups, are told that they are alien creatures. They are challenged to develop a new way of communicating. Members of each group, after some preparation time, should be able to explain (without using English) to the rest of the class who they are, where they are from, and what important message or request they have to share.

Once each group has developed its improvisation, conduct a meeting where all the aliens non-verbally communicate their messages to one another. After each group has presented its message, class members can discuss what they learned about the aliens.

Horrible Thing Makes News

Here are three writing options:

- Students write articles that might accompany this headline: "Extra! Extra! Read All About It: Horrible Thing Invades Village"
- Students encapsulate a story that they told/heard about a visit from an alien creature by writing a newspaper headline in ten words or less.
- Students write letters to the authorities explaining why it is essential to get rid of the creature in the community. They describe the monster and explain in detail the damage it has caused.

Recommended Sources

Baker, K. 1990. *Who Is the Beast?* San Diego, CA: Harcourt Brace.

Bunting, E., and D. Wiesner. 1995. *The Night of the Gargoyles.* New York, NY: David Bennett Books.

Burningham, J. 1978. *Would You Rather …?* London, UK: Jonathan Cape.

Crossley-Holland, K., and E. C. Clark. 2000. *Enchantment: Fairy Tales, Ghost Stories and Tales of Wonder.* London, UK: Orion Children's Books.

Fisher, R. (ed.). 1982. *Amazing Monsters: Verses to Thrill and Chill.* London, UK: Faber and Faber.

Hughes, T. 1968. *The Iron Man.* London, UK: Faber.

Martin, Jr., B., and S. Kellogg. 1999. *A Beasty Tale.* New York, NY: Harcourt Brace & Company.

Singer, M., and G. Grimley. 2001. *Monster Museum.* New York, NY: Hyperion.

Turkle, B. 1981. *Do Not Open.* New York, NY: E. P. Dutton.

Williams, L., and M. Lloyd. 1986. *The Little Old Lady Who Was Not Afraid of Anything.* New York, NY: Thomas Y. Crowell.

Willis, J., and T. Ross. 1990. *Dr. Xargle's Book of Earthlets: An Alien's View of Earth Babies.* London, UK: Red Fox.

Zemach, H., and M. Zemach. 1969. *The Judge.* New York, NY: Farrar, Straus and Giroux.

Student Self-Assessment: Focus on Group Participation

Name: _____ Date: _____

  1. What did you enjoy about the activity?

  2. Were there moments when you worked independently?

  3. Did someone else's idea help you?

  4. Did you ever feel frustrated during the activity?

  5. Was there a leader in your group?

  6. How successfully did you cooperate with other group members?

  7. What did you do if you didn't agree with someone else's idea?

  8. How might this group have worked more efficiently?

  9. What might you do to improve your finished product?

  10. What else would you like to say about working in groups?

4/Animals

Drama is a collaborative group art form where people transform, act, and reflect upon the human condition.

Philip Taylor, *The Drama Classroom:*
Action, Reflection and Transformation (2000, p. 1)

The arts facilitate joyful learning as no other process can, simply because they build on the innate individual and collective desire to express profound ideas and feelings in dance, song, story, or picture. This can be seen by any observer of children as they play, either alone or with others, dramatizing events they have witnessed.

Walter Pitman, *Learning the Arts in*
an Age of Uncertainty (1998, p. 7)

· ·

Source: *The Music of Dolphins*, a novel by Karen Hesse

Theme Overview: *If you could be transformed into any animal, which would you choose to be? How would your world on land, in sea, or in air be different than the one you now know? This dramatheme invites students into the kingdom of four-legged, two-legged, and no-legged creatures. They are given an opportunity to investigate habits and habitats, thoughts and feelings in the shared world of humans and creatures.*

Learning Opportunities
- To develop physical growth through games and movement activities
- To demonstrate an ability to move and control their bodies in space and time, and recognize when it is necessary to sustain concentration in drama and dance
- To represent and interpret main characters by speaking, moving, and writing in role
- To extend understanding of the views of others
- To explore a variety of human emotions
- To explore the world that human and animals share by investigating a novel

· ·

Games: Focus on Physical Activity

Simon Says

The familiar game of "Simon Says" actively involves students in performing actions that the teacher calls out while demonstrating. (For example: "Hands on head," "Bend down," "Clap your hands," "Point to the ceiling.") In this version, no one is eliminated. Anyone who misses a move steps to another part of the room and continues to play the game.

EXTENSION

- Students are asked to become different characters or to perform certain mime activities: for example, crawl like a cat, become a carpenter, climb a ladder, mix a witch's brew, carry an umbrella, growl like a tiger, become the Big Bad Wolf.

Face to Face

Students find a partner and stand face to face. As the teacher calls out "face to face" or "back to back," partners respond to each direction. When the teacher calls out "change," everyone, including the teacher, seeks a new partner and stands either face to face or back to back. The one person who is left out becomes the new caller. (Since an odd number of players is needed to play the game effectively, the teacher can participate in the game accordingly.)

EXTENSION

- Repeat the game several times. Once students are familiar with it, the caller can shout out different instructions, such as "toe to toe," "side to side," "knee to knee," "ear to ear."

Safari

Students sit in a circle to form a jungle. They number off from one to five and give themselves the following identities: 1 - cheetah; 2 - elephant; 3 - ape; 4 - rhino; 5 - zebra. The teacher calls out an animal name, for example, "zebra." All zebras then run around the outside of the circle and get back "home" as quickly as possible. The last person to reach home becomes the caller for the next round. Once students are familiar with the game, the teacher can call the names of two animals. When the word "safari" is called, all players must run around the circle and return home.

Tortoise and Hare

The group sits or stands in a circle. One ball represents the tortoise, and a second ball, the hare. The ball representing the tortoise is passed around the circle in a clockwise direction from player to player. The ball representing the hare can be thrown around the circle in any direction. The object of this game is for the hare to catch the tortoise. This occurs when one player is passed the tortoise ball and thrown the hare ball at the same time. The game is then repeated.

- To make the game more complicated, a third ball is introduced as a second hare. Eventually, a fourth ball, representing a second tortoise, is introduced.

Building a Zoo

In this activity, students work spontaneously in a variety of group situations. They work with different people in each situation and should work with the same class member only once. The students' task is to create a zoo by using their bodies to represent various animals. On a signal, students work

- alone to make a mosquito,
- with a partner to make a swan,
- in groups of three to make a tarantula,
- in groups of four to make a giraffe,
- in groups of five to make an elephant,
- in groups of six to invent a "new" animal for the zoo

EXTENSION

- On a signal, students re-form groups to create animals. They are instructed to make the sound of the animal, move in slow motion as the animal (no sounds), move and make the sounds of the animal.

Drama Exploration: Focus on Movement

Letters and Numbers

This game requires students to interpret instructions imaginatively at the same time that they use their body for flexible movement. There are several variations that can be used.

- A letter is called out — students attempt to make their bodies look like the letter (they can do this on their own or with a partner).
- Students make the letter look a certain way according to instructions, for example, that the letter be as wide as possible or lowercase and as small as possible.
- In groups of three or four, students answer questions by using their bodies (e.g., What is the total age of your group?).

Writing Names without Pencils

Students work imaginatively to interpret instructions and develop movement skills. To begin, they write their names in the air. They are then directed to use only part of their bodies (e.g., their left ear, their right shoulder) to write their names. The activity can be varied through requests for large and small movements, the use of imaginary equipment (e.g., a feather, a hose), and name variations (e.g., writing their last name or the name of a friend).

- Instead of their names, students spell different words.
- The game is done as a mirror activity, in which students copy a partner's movements.
- Students send messages to partners by writing in a mutually shared space.

Move Along!

This activity is best done in a large space, such as a gym. Encourage students to interpret the instructions in their own way and not be swayed from their interpretations by their friends' movements. Ask them to move from one side of the room to another in these ways:

- in slow motion
- with one foot and one hand on the floor
- with no feet touching the floor
- with their head on the floor
- backwards
- in a swirling motion
- like a kangaroo
- like a spider
- like a monster
- in as few moves as possible
- silently
- as if being chased
- as if moving through a thick fog
- as if they were in a blender
- as if their feet were tied together
- as if the floor was made of glue
- as if the floor was made of hot sand
- attached to a partner

EXTENSION

- Students, working in groups of four or five, tangle themselves up into a knot and solve the problem of moving across the room as a group.

Walk This Way!

The following activities develop basic movement skills. Students work in their own spaces as the teacher calls out various movements for them to perform.

Walk
- through a field of tall weeds • on a pile of feathers • through puddles • on a faraway planet • on a hot sidewalk

Run
- using as much/as little space as possible • as if you were an animal • as if it were winter/summer • as if being chased

Crawl
- along top of a narrow, high bridge • as if collecting ants • with heads towards the sky • through a tiny, tight doorway

Roll
- like a red carpet being laid before a king • like a log rolling down a bumpy hill • like dough being made into a pizza

Jump
- as high as possible • in fast/slow motion • as far as possible • in teeny, tiny jumps • like popcorn • like a soccer player

Twist
- like a milkshake being made in a blender • like leaves falling from the tree • on an amusement ride

Turn
- around on the spot • with one foot on the ground • with one hand on the floor • like a bottle top being opened • using different parts of the body

Bounce
- very high/very low • like a rubber ball • like a very heavy ball • in many directions

Fill in the Spaces

Students work in pairs. Partner A begins by making a movement that fills as much space as possible (e.g., arms spread wide, leg pointing forward) and then freezes. Partner B must then assume a position that "fills in the spaces" that partner A has left. Partner B then freezes into this position. Partner A then unfreezes and tries to connect himself or herself to partner B, by filling in the spaces and so on. This activity is best done to slow music. Encourage students to use as many levels as possible.

EXTENSIONS

- Have the students work in groups of four or five. Each student is given a number and, therefore, should freeze into position according to that number.
- Each student decides, on his or her own, when to thaw out.
- The students perform the fill-in-the-spaces exercise, but are given a title or a word that should influence their movements (e.g., sunshine, change, storm, garden, hate, anger, growth).

Mirrors

Mirror exercises work well when introduced with rather slow music. Some suggestions are *Chariots of Fire* by Vangelis, *Gymnopedies* by Erik Satie, "Pachelbel's Canon, " and "Memory" from the musical *Cats*.

Students work in pairs, with one partner becoming the "mirror." The other person stands in front of the mirror and moves in slow motion, using only hands and arms at first. As the mirror becomes more confident in copying movements, the movements could be expanded to include the whole body. The students may change roles from time to time, so that each gets practice being both the mirror and the reflected person.

To begin the mirror exercises, it is suggested that students sit facing each other. As they become more familiar with the nature of the exercises, they can stand, move, and eventually explore other spaces in the room. You can move the students through the exercises, perhaps suggesting which part of the body to move and which levels to explore.

EXTENSIONS

- Have all the students freeze. On a signal, all the A's thaw, find a new partner B, and become a mirror reflection as the exercise continues.
- The students form groups of four and number themselves 1–4. Each time you call a number, that person becomes the leader for the rest of the group to mirror.

- The students work in groups of seven or eight. One person is asked to face away from the group or perhaps leave the room. The group then chooses a leader who will conduct the mirror exercise. Once the group has begun mirroring, the person who left returns and guesses who he or she thinks the leader is. The students who are the mirror reflections should be careful not to look directly at the leader in order to make the guessing more difficult. Also, the group should be allowed to continue the exercise for one or two minutes before the person tries to guess who the leader is. This game might be more successful if the students remain seated.
- Repeat the above exercise with the whole group or by having two groups together. Eventually the whole group could sit in a circle and perhaps try to fool you about who is the leader.

Shadows

This movement activity is similar to the mirror exercise except that the students sit or stand one behind the other in a line. As the person in front moves, the person standing behind the leader "shadows" the movements.

Flocking

In this movement improvisation, the group works collectively as they shift from following to leading one another's movement. The effect is similar to mirroring in the pacing and movement quality. Three or more people can be used in a flocking exercise. A theme, character, concept, or journey can be interpreted through flocking.

1. One person is chosen to lead and faces one wall.
2. The three remaining students face the same wall, behind the leader.
3. Each of the four members stand apart, as if to make a square.
4. When the leader begins to move, the others shadow the leader's movement.
5. The leader can choose to rotate left or right.
6. The person who is now in front assumes the leadership role.
7. The activity continues, with group members shifting around the circle, changing directions spontaneously.

A Drama Structure: *The Music of Dolphins* by Karen Hesse

Phase One: Let's Shake Hands

The students walked randomly about the room and shook hands with people they met. On a signal, they were advised that they could let go of someone's hand that they were shaking, only if they joined hands with another person. The group continued moving about the space. No player should have had a free hand.

The activity was repeated several times, with students receiving new instructions about various ways to greet people:

- greeting in slow motion
- making eye contact as they connected with a new partner
- using different levels as they moved about the room
- reaching out to someone not close to them
- greeting to the accompaniment of a slow piece of music

At the completion of the activity, students discussed reasons why people would shake hands and then depart. What might the story/context be for the game?

Phase Two: Transformations

Students moved about the room. When names of animals were called out, they stopped and, using their bodies, transformed into various creatures (e.g., shark, eel, sea turtle, octopus, tuna, dolphin). The game continued with students thawing out and then moving about the room until another animal name was called out. If a name was repeated, students returned to the spots where they first transformed into that animal.

Phase Three: Building Narrative

Students were given the photo image of a child and a dolphin. Working in pairs, they discussed the image and made hypotheses about the scene. The discussion was framed around the following questions: How did this child come to swim on the dolphin's back? What image might have been depicted in photographs that were taken at some future time (ten minutes, one hour, that night)?

Once the partners decided on a story of the child and the dolphin, they were instructed to retell the story in three frozen images that would represent three photographs taken sequentially. The class shared their images and then discussed the story that they predicted about this child.

Phase Four: A Context for Drama

The students were given an excerpt from *The Music of Dolphins* (page 64). In this newspaper article, readers first learn about the wild child. To prepare for the drama, the class discussed the information that they knew from reading this text and raised questions that came to mind about the life of the girl.

Phase Five: Improvisation

Students met in role as a group of scientists at the Institute for Behavioral Research. The teacher appeared in role as the helicopter pilot and welcomed any questions from the expert scientists about the rescue mission.

Working out of role, the students discussed new information that was learned in the improvisation.

Phase Six: Planning

a) Students met in small groups and discussed plans to deal with the wild child, Mila: What procedures should be taken to prepare her to live in a civilized manner? The students, as behavior scientists, were invited to consider the following:

- What food should she be given?
- What activities should she be invited to do?
- What kind of environment would be the most appropriate for her?
- What objects should be given to her?
- How might she best learn language?
- Who might she best interact with?

Wild Child Found on Island Off Cuba

MIAMI, FL, Dec. 5—"I thought she was a mermaid at first," said Lieutenant Junior Grade Monica Stone. "Her hair hung down to her feet and she was covered with seaweed." On closer examination the flight crew on the Coast Guard Jay Hawk realized they'd spotted not a mermaid but a human child.

Their mission started as a routine surveillance flight over the Cay Sal bank in the waters between Florida and Cuba. The crew, composed of Stone, pilot Nicholas Fisk, and flight mechanic Gary Barnett, had flown hundreds of search-and-rescue missions over this section of water. But this mission was unlike any they'd flown before.

After the initial observation of the child, the crew radioed Miami and awaited clearance to land. Hovering above, they videotaped the girl. "Gary threw the pump can out to her on a parachute. Pump cans hold food, blankets, first aid. Most people run toward them. This girl ran away, hiding in the mangroves. She had this really weird way of moving, like the ground was rolling under her feet. Gary climbed down and walked toward her, holding out his hand."

"She was so strange," said Barnett. "The way she acted. More like an animal than a human."

Once they got her aboard the helicopter, Stone wrapped the naked girl in a blanket. "She was making a high-pitched cry, like a seagull," said Stone. "Her respiration was odd, popping out of her, like breathing was something she had to remember to do."

Stone, a communications and public relations specialist, speaks fluent English, Spanish, and French. The child either couldn't or wouldn't respond to efforts to communicate in any language.

Her height and body development suggest a girl somewhere between the ages of eleven and sixteen years, said Stone. Her weight, in the vicinity of one hundred pounds, is at least ten percent hair.

"Most refugees we pick up look as if they've been at sea a couple of days. Their eyes are bloodshot. They're dehydrated," said Barnett. "But they still look human. This girl was streaked with salt. There were barnacles growing on her, for crying out loud. The condition of her skin — she had circular scars all over her face and body — she had to be living in the sea a long time."

"Mila [the name given her by the Coast Guard crew] is definitely human, but there's something about her, something wild," Stone said.

The Immigration and Naturalization Service; the Bahamian, Haitian, and Cuban governments; and a team of medical specialists working under grants issued by the National Institute of Mental Health are disputing custody of the newly discovered wild child, the second such discovery in as many months.

True wild children are a rare occurrence, said Dr. Elizabeth Beck, research professor of cognitive and neural systems at Boston University. "Feral children are an invaluable resource for studying the role language and socialization play in the making of a human being."

From *The Music of Dolphins*
by Karen Hesse

b) After one week, the teacher, in role as a behavior scientist, met with students. The improvised meeting focused on discussing Mila's progress. Each of the scientist groups prepared a report to discuss Mila's development. They addressed the topics of her behavior, procedures taken to "educate" her, their concerns about her, and next steps for her learning.

Phase Seven: Mila's Dreams

As Mila learned to communicate, she was given music and art materials to help her represent her thoughts. In this phase of the drama, the students worked towards recapturing Mila's world through music and movement. In small groups they prepared a dance drama that represents Mila's dreams. They considered questions such as these: What does she remember about her life with the dolphins? What are her concerns about the future? How does she feel about the people she has met? What makes her happy? What makes her fearful?

Drama Convention: Dance Drama

Dance drama is movement with the interpretation of a piece of music, a series of sounds, a story, or an emotional theme. The conflict or issues inspired by a drama context are conveyed through the patterns and rhythms of dance. Dance drama can be simple, with each student interpreting a story independently, or it can be more complex, with groups of students telling a story through stylized movement. A dance drama is most often supported by music, although sound exploration, narrated text, chanting, costumes, or masks can enrich the presentation.

Phase Eight: Tensions

Students considered these issues.

- Should Mila return to the world of the dolphins? Progress has been too slow. She has deteriorated. She has expressed a strong desire to return to the family that raised her, where she can be independent and happy.
- Mila's father has sent a letter explaining how his daughter came to be abandoned. It's not possible for Mila's father to come and get her. Should she be returned to her father?
- Another "wild child" has been discovered. The child has been experiencing much less progress than Mila. How can Mila be "used" to enrich the life of the new child?
- Mila needs music to enrich her life. What would happen to Mila if music were no longer available to her? What if music was forbidden to her because it was interfering with her progress? How could the authorities be convinced that music should be part of Mila's development?

Phase Nine: Planning a Documentary

Drama Convention: Documentaries

Preparing a documentary allows students to examine a theme, issue, or story from different viewpoints using a variety of drama conventions. As they work in groups to plan and prepare a documentary, students come to understand the power of using the media to inform or persuade audiences about a topic or issue. When dealing with historical or news events, students have an opportunity to gather, interpret, and deliver information at both a personal and societal level.

It was decided that a documentary film would be made about wild children. Students worked in small groups to plan what scenes might appear in the documentary and consider such questions as these:

- Why is Mila's story of interest to the world?
- What are the various points of view that could be depicted in the film?
- Who might be interviewed?
- Who might tell Mila's story?
- What scenes of the dolphin world might be shown?
- What factual information about dolphins needs to be included?
- What artifacts (art, writing, toys, memorabilia) from Mila's life might be used in the film?

The way in which they shared their ideas was much like a producers' meeting.

Each group presented one scene that members felt should be included in the documentary. Videotaping the work was an option.

Beyond the Drama

Writing in Role
Here are three options:

- Students consider who might write Mila a letter should she go back to the sea to live with the dolphins. They need to determine what information, thoughts, and feelings should be included.
- The media have been covering Mila's progress. Students prepare a report that might appear in scientific journals about Mila's story and development.
- Students write at least one journal entry that Mila might make as she learns to use English and express her feelings about her treatment at the Institute.

Exploring Visual Arts
Here, students think visually:

- Students consider this question: If Mila were to be given a box of paints, a chunk of clay/Plasticine, or a pile of construction paper, what art might she create to represent her memories of the sea world she left behind?

- Using a variety of media, students create a mural of the sea world that might be painted on Mila's bedroom wall.
- Students determine what Mila's room at the Institute might look like. What kind of furniture would she feel comfortable with? What objects might appear in the room? What drawings or posters might be on the wall? They could sketch the room.

Dancing the Story

Students retell Mila's story using movement. The class can be divided into groups representing Mila's past/present/future.

Assessing Actions in Role

Mila has returned to the sea, so the scientists/doctors meet to discuss the implications of their actions. Students in role consider what they could learn from Mila's situation that would help them in the development of other young people with special needs.

Communicating by Letter

Mila has learned about her father from a letter (see *The Music of Dolphins*, p. 58). In pairs, one student plays Mila and another, a companion. Mila discusses her feelings about the news and contemplates the future. Following the improvisation, the pairs compose a letter that Mila could send her father.

Snippets of the letter can be read to someone representing the father. The father is then put in the hot seat to share his feelings about his daughter.

Recommended Sources

Cooper, S., and W. Hutton. 1986. *The Selkie Girl*. New York, NY: Margaret K. McElderry Books.

Doherty, B. (ed.). 1998. *The Forsaken Merman: And Other Story Poems*. London, UK: Hodder Children's Books.

Farris, D. 1994. *In Dolphin Time*. New York, NY: Four Winds Press.

Gerstein, Mordicai. 1998. *The Wild Boy*. New York, NY: Farrar, Straus, Giroux. (Also: *Victor*, a novel)

Hesse, K. 1996. *The Music of Dolphins*. New York, NY: Scholastic Inc.

Martin, R., and D. Shannon. 1995. *The Boy Who Lived with the Seals*. New York, NY: G. P. Putnam's Sons.

O'Dell, S. 1960. *Island of the Blue Dolphins*. New York, NY: Yearling Books.

Rylant, C. 1998. *The Islander*. New York, NY: DK Publishing.

Windham, S. (ed.). 1994. *The Mermaid and Other Sea Poems*. New York, NY: Orchard Books.

Assessment: Focus on Movement

Name: _____ Date: _____

Does the student …	Always	Sometimes	Never
enjoy playing physical games?	❏	❏	❏
enjoy participating in movement activities?	❏	❏	❏
work well with partners, in small groups, and with the whole class?	❏	❏	❏
treat and support others?	❏	❏	❏
express ideas using the body?	❏	❏	❏
appear energetic?	❏	❏	❏
comply with instructions?	❏	❏	❏
appear willing to take risks?	❏	❏	❏

Comments:

_____

_____

_____

_____

5/Relationships

Always in my teaching I push for those moments when the class begins to see itself differently — when they have opportunities to write and speak a new classroom script.

Kathleen Lundy, in Orbit, Spring 2002

. . . .

Source: *I Met a Bully on the Hill*, **a script by Martha Brooks and Maureen Hunter**

Theme Overview: *In this dramatheme, students have an opportunity to explore the complexities of trusting, negotiating, problem-solving, cooperating, and living with others. By creating and exploring the identities and dilemmas of fictional characters seeking a safe place to belong, they can have a better understanding of the relationships in their own lives.*

Learning Opportunities
- To negotiate and cooperate with others in the creation of drama work
- To sustain a role with increasing confidence and competence
- To identify their own feelings and reactions in various situations, and to compare them with those of a character they have portrayed
- To practise role playing in order to better understand the thoughts, feelings, and motivations of others
- To understand the motivations behind bullying behavior
- To prepare those who are being victimized by bullies to better deal with their situations

. . . .

Games: Focus on Cooperation

Cooperative Tag

In this game of tag, everyone is "It" at the same time that everyone is being chased. The object of the game is for a player to tag someone before being tagged. When tagged, the player freezes and stands with his or her legs spread apart. To be "defrosted," the frozen player must have another person crawl through his or her legs. Confusion may result in who was tagged first — sorting out such problems develops cooperative skills.

VARIATIONS

- In Elbow Tag, "It" can tag someone only if she or he has not linked arms with another player. When tagged, the player becomes "lt."
- In Blob Tag, "It" is an amoeba who tries to tag other players. If tagged, the player links arms with the amoeba and becomes part of "It." Other players can be tagged only by the free arm of players on either end of the growing amoeba. The object of the game is to tag all players.

I Packed My Bag 1: An Oral Game

Students sit in a circle of eight to ten players. The first player says, "I packed my bag and in it I put a toothbrush." The second player says, "I packed my bag and in it I put a toothbrush and a violin." The third player packs a toothbrush, a violin, and something new, for example, a banana. Each player repeats in order all that has gone before and adds a new object. The game can continue for several minutes, so that each player names one, two, or three objects.

EXTENSION

- To make the game more challenging, have players add objects in alphabetical order, objects whose names begin with the same letter, objects whose names have two syllables, or objects whose names are accompanied by an adjective.

I Packed My Bag 2: A Mime Game

The rules are the same as the traditional "I Packed My Bag" game, but instead of saying "toothbrush," for example, players act out an activity that involves that noun. As examples, "toothbrush" may become the brushing of one's teeth, and "violin," the playing of the instrument. Each player repeats in order all that has gone before and adds a new mime.

Musical Newspapers

Explain to the class that the principle of this game is to "save" as many people as possible. To begin, about 12–15 pieces of newspaper are laid flat on the floor. Some fast music is played, and the class moves around until the music stops. Players rush in to find a piece of newspaper to stand on. When the music resumes, students continue to move about the room until the music stops and they land on a piece of paper. Each time the game is replayed, the number of papers is reduced. As the papers become fewer, it is obvious that in order to "save" others, members must devise ways of using their bodies to hold more people on the reduced number of papers.

Atom

As the teacher calls out instructions such as "Skip," "Jog," or whatever, students move about the room as directed. Whenever the teacher calls out a number, for example, "Atom 3!", groups must be formed with that number of people in them. On "Atom 1!" everybody freezes in a "hugging" position. The teacher may call any number and may repeat a number that has already been called. If people are left over, they may form a smaller group, but cannot join a complete group.

EXTENSION

- This game can be played with the students moving about to fast music. Give specific instructions about how the groups should form themselves: taking as much space as possible, using the least amount of space possible, making a beautiful sculpture, creating an alien creature, all connecting without touching hands, and connecting without feet touching the floor.

Where Do I Belong?

On a signal from the teacher, students sort themselves along a straight line

- from shortest to tallest, with the shortest person at the head of the line
- according to birthdays, with January birthdays at the head of the line
- according to age, with the youngest person at the head of the line
- according to shoe size, with the smallest shoe size at the head of the line
- according to their street numbers, with the smallest number at the head of the line (If students share the same number, they stand side by side.)
- in alphabetical order using first names only. (If students share the same name, they can stand side by side.)

Family Reunion

This game has students working in flexible groups. Sets of four to six cards, depending on the number of students in the class, are printed with family names: for example, Father Jones, Mother Jones, Sister Jones, and Brother Jones; Father Stein, Mother Stein, Sister Stein, Brother Stein, Cousin Stein, and Grandmother Stein. Each student is given a card. Students wander the room and exchange cards with anyone they meet. On a signal, they first look at their cards and then find their families. Once all members are present, families retire to one corner of the room and create a tableau representing a photo in the family album. The game can be repeated.

EXTENSIONS

- After playing the game several times, students remain with one family to create three pictures for the family album. Captions to accompany the photos can be suggested (e.g., Our Family Vacation, Happy Birthday, At the Amusement Park, We Won!, An Embarrassing Moment).
- New groups are formed by having all fathers, mothers, sisters, brothers, cousins, and grandmothers meet for a group picture.
- Students combine with another group to create a photo with eight or twelve family members. They decide who will be in the family photo.

Encourage each student to take another role than the one she or he played in the original photograph.

- Tell students that not all family pictures are displayed in a photo album. Ask them to imagine that a family has hidden one picture, perhaps because it reveals a sad time, a disturbing episode, or an unexpected surprise! Students, in their family groups, discuss the story behind the picture and create a frozen tableau to depict the moment. They bring the photos to life by revealing their inner thoughts. This more sophisticated activity could develop into a dramatic exploration of family relationships.

Drama Exploration: Focus on Character

News Report

a) Each student clips a picture of one person from a magazine or newspaper. The pictures should feature people who interest the students in some way, perhaps because of their expression or pose, or because of the setting of the photographs. To make the activity more valid, students should choose pictures of unknown people, rather than celebrities.

b) Students become media reporters. Their job is to interview the people featured in the photographs. They think of five or six questions they would like to ask of the person whose picture they have chosen. Once students have prepared their questions, they choose three questions that they believe will yield the most interesting information.

c) Students work with a partner to conduct an interview. One student role-plays the part of a person in a photograph; the second, the part of a reporter. Afterwards, they switch roles.

d) After the improvisation, students work independently to write their newspaper or magazine articles. If necessary, they replay their roles in order to generate more information for their articles.

e) Students are told that their two characters are both going to appear in a newspaper's front page article. What do these characters have in common? Why might their story be on the front page of a newspaper? What headline will they use for their article? Together, each pair of students plans, as reporters, a story that they think might appear in a featured news report. They then create a frozen tableau that represents the front page photograph of the newspaper article.

f) As a final activity, students conduct a news conference where each pair of students shares their news story. Pairs present their stories in role as reporters or as characters from the pictures. In the latter instance, the rest of the class assumes the role of newspaper reporters conducting a group interview.

EXTENSIONS

- Partners write the newspaper article as it might appear on the front page of the newspaper. They include a headline and picture that might appear on the front page.
- Partners write their newspaper article as an interview. They use some or all of the questions they prepared for their interview.

- Partners share their article with another pair of students. Groups of four brainstorm what the four characters have in common.

A Day in the Life

Drama Convention: A Day in the Life

This strategy is useful in drama, particularly when a character is faced with a problem she or he must solve. Played in pairs or in small groups, it helps students recognize the roles we assume in various situations. One person should be assigned the central role; his or her partner or group members will switch roles throughout the improvisation.

The following scenarios that show the day in the life of one character are outlined to the students. They choose one to explore, making a decision about who will play the central character.

Character 1: *Teenager*
— eating breakfast with his or her family
— meeting friends at school
— discussing lackadaisical work habits with his or her teacher(s)
— applying for an after-school job
— meeting the parents of a girl or boy friend

Character 2: *Parent*
— eating breakfast with his or her family, complaining about the news
— asking his or her boss for a raise
— sitting in the cafeteria with his or her friends and a new employee
— meeting a son's or daughter's teachers
— discussing a broken curfew with a son or daughter

Character 3: *Teacher*
— getting her little boy ready for school
— talking to the principal about lack of supplies
— visiting a parent who is ill
— speaking to a student about his or her behavior
— talking to a professor about a poor grade he or she received on an essay

After experiencing one of the situations, students discuss how we change roles according to who we are with and where we interact. As well, they discuss how the concept of self varies from situation to situation and how we use techniques to put other people at ease. Students could identify times when they feel most like themselves and times when they feel least like themselves.

EXTENSION

- Students work in different groups. In each group, one member plays the same central character. This character meets different people throughout the day and may discuss his or her problem with some or all of them.

A Drama Structure: *I Met a Bully on the Hill*
by Martha Brooks and Maureen Hunter

The following events were implemented over several days to help students explore the issue of bullying. A few sources related to the topic (see Recommended Sources at the end of the chapter) were introduced throughout the week for drama exploration. This work also helped provide contexts for writing in role, which were used to reflect on roles explored in the drama and served as a source for further drama development.

Lesson One: What Is Bullying?

To prompt a discussion about bullying, students completed a questionnaire independently (see page 75). After sharing their answers in small groups, the class discussed responses, stories, and issues related to bullies and victims. The discussion was framed around these questions:

- What is a bully?
- What do you think motivates young people to bully?
- How can someone prepare themselves for the possibility of encountering a bully?

A Definition of Bullying: Students worked in groups to write a dictionary definition of the word "bullying" using the following context:

A new dictionary is about to be published, but "bully" has yet to be defined. Students, as dictionary editors, have been called upon for their input. They were given file cards to write their definitions of "bully." They next worked with a partner to compare definitions.

These options could also be provided.

- Partners could work together to create a single definition.
- To make the activity more challenging, students could work in small groups to collaborate on a definition. The definition had to be exactly twenty words long.
- Tell students that the new dictionary will be strictly visual so that all definitions must be represented without words. Students create an image or design to represent bullying.

Lesson Two: Improvising from a Source

a) Students were provided with a picture similar to that on page 76 to have them develop the roles of both a victim and a bully. Before beginning the drama, students discussed what they learned by examining this image and hypothesized the story that might accompany the scene.

b) As a class, students created a Role on the Wall chart for both of the characters in the picture (see page 77). On the outside of each figure, we recorded words that described the external appearance of the character. On the inside of each figure, we recorded words that described the feelings that this character might have.

c) Students worked in pairs to re-create the images of the bully and of the victim that were depicted in this scene. They were told to create the images as precisely as possible, considering spacing, gestures, facial expressions, etc. On a signal, the frozen image was depicted.

A Questionnaire about Bullying

Answer each of the following statements by circling whether you *Agree* or *Disa*

1. Bullies are mostly boys.	**Agree**	**Disagree**
2. Bullies have friends.	**Agree**	**Disagree**
3. Most bullies hit their victims.	**Agree**	**Disagree**
4. Bullies are cowards.	**Agree**	**Disagree**
5. Bullies select victims that they are sure won't fight back.	**Agree**	**Disagree**
6. I can tell a person is a bully from the person's looks.	**Agree**	**Disagree**
7. It is important to ignore bullies.	**Agree**	**Disagree**
8. It's tattling if you report a bully to an adult.	**Agree**	**Disagree**
9. The best way to deal with a bully is by getting even.	**Agree**	**Disagree**
10. Bullying is a normal way of growing up.	**Agree**	**Disagree**

11. One word to describe a bully is _____

12. One word to describe a victim is _____

13. Here is my picture of a bully.

Drama Convention: Role on the Wall

A central role that is to be explored in the drama is represented in picture form, diagram, or outline on a chart, which is put on the wall. Students reflect on the thoughts, feelings, and qualities that are significant to this character and add words or statements. Information about the role is added as the drama is introduced and progresses. This role can be adopted by students in the improvisation.

Consider the following options for recording information on the Role on the Wall diagram.

1. What are the inner characteristics and external characteristics of this character?
2. What are the different views that others — the community, family members, the character himself/herself — might have of this character?
3. What is known or not known about the character's life?

- The activity was repeated with partners reversing roles.
- The activity was repeated once again, reversing roles, so that partners were depicting the image that they originally began with.
- Using the convention of Voices in the Head, the students, in a still position, were invited to speak aloud a thought that their characters might have at this time.

Drama Convention: Voices in the Head

This strategy is useful in helping students reflect on the many facets that a character in a drama must face in making a choice. Students represent the possible conflicting thoughts of the character at the moment a decision is made. The voices become the character's conscience that gives the person advice, forcing him or her to make a moral or life-threatening choice.

Voices in the Head helps the students to become more aware of the complexity of a problem and allows them to influence the imminent action. As students call out their thoughts, they slow down the action of the drama, adding tension to the moment.

---

d) Students created an improvisation that would bring this scene to life. To prepare for the scene, they discussed the relationship of the two characters and explored why these characters might be having this conversation.
e) The improvisation was repeated with partners switching roles. The characters could incorporate some of the conversation from the previous improvisation. To replay the scene, students were asked to consider the use of spacing and gesturing. How would the characters move during the improvisation? Would eye contact be used? How might their voices be used to depict the argument?

f) The students playing victims in each scene remained standing. The teacher interviewed these characters to learn more about their situation:

- How would you describe the bully?
- Why did this person pick on you?
- Has the person bullied you before?
- Did this person listen to any of your arguments?
- What attempts did you make to help the bully understand your point of view?
- Were you expecting this person to bully you or were you surprised?
- Are you going to tell anyone about this situation?
- Who do you think might be able to help you?
- What do you think is going to happen when you meet this bully again?

g) Students worked in pairs. Those who were the bullies were invited to assume the role of the victim. Those who were the victims assumed the role of helper (e.g., family member, neighbor, best friend, school counsellor, someone else who has been bullied by this person). Students improvised a situation where the victims tried to get help. The victims might not have felt comfortable talking about the situation at first and might have chosen to reveal limited information. Those listening to the victims worked towards offering advice and reaching a solution for the them.

These options could also be pursued:

- Working in small groups, students could brainstorm a list of suggestions that might be given to someone who is confronted by a bully. The students could share their thoughts with another group and prioritize their list with the most appropriate strategies.
- In role as a school counsellor or advice columnist, students could write a letter to the victim, offering suggestions for ways to handle the bullying problem. See "Ways to Handle Put-Downs and Bullying."
- A class discussion could be held about ways to handle a bully. The discussion could be framed around the pros and cons of each suggestion.

Lesson Three: Working with a Script

The students worked with the excerpt from *I Met a Bully on the Hill* (page 79) in the following ways:

a) The script was read aloud as a class. The teacher read the part of Raymond; the students read the part of J.J.
b) The activity was repeated, reversing roles.
c) Students worked in pairs to read the script aloud. Each student had a chance to play Raymond so that the scene was read twice. The first time the script was read, Raymond was invited to be a calm, quiet character and J.J. was angry. The second time the script was read, Raymond was instructed to be angry, and J.J. was instructed to be calm and quiet.
d) The conversation was repeated. This time, students did not read the script aloud, but improvised the scene. To begin, J.J. moved away from Raymond and quietly approached him when ready. Each pair was invited to continue the dialogue for a moment or two. How did J.J. react to Raymond's threat?

Ways to Handle Put-Downs and Bullying

1. Ask a question.
2. Repeat back information used in the argument.
3. Identify the feelings of the bully.
4. Agree.
5. Make a joke.
6. Change the subject.
7. Ask for advice.
8. Use an "I" statement.
9. Ignore.
10. Leave.
11. Name the bullying behavior and remind the bully that it is against school rules.
12. Report the behavior.

I Met a Bully on the Hill: *from* Scene Three

by Martha Brooks and Maureen Hunter

RAYMOND: Moooo! (*Moves in on her beaming broadly.*) Well, look who's here. Little Miss Cowgirl. With her cute little bow. (*Fingers it.*)

J.J.: Stop it. (*J.J. moves to leave. Raymond blocks her.*)
Let me past.

RAYMOND: Hey, I'd like to. Honest. But what can I do? You're on my hill.

J.J.: It's not your hill.

RAYMOND: J.J., J.J., J.J. What am I going to do with you? You can't seem to get things through your head. Maybe that's because you're from the country. So I'm going to ask you one more time. (*Leans into her.*) Whose hill is this?

J.J.: Nobody's.

RAYMOND: It's my hill. Isn't it?

J.J.: I guess so.

RAYMOND: I can't hear you.

J.J.: (*louder*) It's your hill.

RAYMOND: Very good.

J.J.: I told you. I have to use it.

RAYMOND: You have to use it. Well now, that creates a little problem. See — nobody uses my hill. Hmmmmmm. I got it! I'll charge you rent.

e) Using the convention of forum theatre, the scene was improvised using two volunteers. The class made suggestions on how the characters might move and what they might say.

Drama Convention: Forum Theatre

In Forum Theatre, a situation is enacted by any number of players while the rest of the group observes the action. Observers can step in and take over roles, or add suggestions to make the scene more authentic. Forum Theatre allows students to explore a variety of attitudes to an event as they work through it in drama. In Forum Theatre, the audience can stop the action from time to time in order to make suggestions about characters' dialogue and behaviors. Scenes are repeated so that suggestions can be implemented and analyzed.

Problem Solving: Working in small groups, the students brainstormed plans for J.J. to handle the bully on the hill. The class then created a conscience alley, a strategy that Jonothan Neelands and Tony Goode introduced me to. This strategy is useful for making public some of the conflicts and dilemmas that a character in a drama might experience. It is also known as "Corridor of Voices," since characters move through a corridor formed by students who speak a character's thoughts.

Drama Convention: Conscience Alley, or Corridor of Voices

The class forms two facing lines, thus forming an alley. The teacher (or student) in role represents a protagonist from the drama. As the character walks slowly down the alley, the students represent the character's conscience to show his or her thoughts about making a choice. The voices can offer advice, warnings, or quotes from earlier in the drama. As the character reaches the end of the alley/corridor, he or she decides what course of action to take.

Students arranged themselves in two lines, facing each other, with one student assigned the role of J.J. The students were told that the next day J.J. had to walk by the hill again, aware of Raymond's threat of charging her rent money to walk past it. As J.J. left school to walk home, many thoughts ran through her head. As she passed through the human alley, students spoke these thoughts aloud. When J.J. reached the end of the alley, she met Raymond. A short improvisation which dealt with J.J. making a decision about paying the rent followed.

After the improvisation, students discussed how J.J. handled the situation and brainstormed ways to handle a bully.

Beyond the Drama

The following opportunities are suggestions for writing in role while exploring this dramatheme. Students can assume the identity of a character that has been explored within the drama, or they can respond in writing to a character from a poem, picture book, or novel in role.

Writing to an Advice Columnist
Students write a letter to an advice columnist, describing the problem and articulating the victim's feelings.

Extension: Students exchange letters and write a letter back as the advice columnist, offering suggestions about ways to handle the situation.

Reflecting on a Bullying Incident
Students are invited to write a fictitious diary entry from that character's point of view where he/she describes an incident and feelings about the incident.

Writing Persuasively
Students write a letter of advice to a bully from someone who has been bullied. In role, students explain their feelings and try to persuade the bully to end that behavior.

Making an Apology
In role as a bully, students write a letter of apology. In the letter students should try to explain their behavior, offering reflections on why they think they behaved the way they did.

Preparing a Guide Book
Students working alone or in small groups prepare a guide book entitled *How to Deal with Bullies*. Each page of the booklet should offer a recommended suggestion and could be illustrated.

Continuing the Script
Students work with a partner to prepare a short script as a response to an improvisation between a bully and a victim. For example, they could continue the scene that opens Scene Three of *I Met a Bully on the Hill* by writing the rest of the conversation between J.J. and Raymond.

Recommended Sources

Picture Books
Angelou, M., and J-M. Basquiat. 1993. *Life Doesn't Frighten Me at All*. New York, NY: Stewart, Tabori & Chang.
Browne, A. 1985. *Willy the Champ*. New York, NY: Alfred A. Knopf. (Also: *Willy the Wimp* and *Willy and Hugh*)
Cannon, J. 2000. *Crickwing*. San Diego, CA: Harcourt Brace.
Cosby, B. 1997. *The Meanest Thing to Say*. New York, NY: Scholastic Inc.
Howe, J. 1996. *Pinky and Rex and the Bully*. New York, NY: Atheneum.
Lester, H. 1999. *Hooway for Wodney Wat*. Boston, MA: Houghton Mifflin.
Nickle, J. 1999. *The Ant Bully*. New York, NY: Scholastic Inc.
Rosenberg. L. 1991. *Monster Mama*. Boston, MA: Little, Brown.
Wells, R. 1973. *Benjamin and Tulip*. New York, NY: Dial Books.

Novels

Bloor, E. 1997. *Tangerine*. New York, NY: Scholastic Inc.

Clements, A. 2001. *Jake Drake Bully Buster*. New York, NY: Aladdin.

Conly, J. L. 1998. *While No One Was Watching*. New York, NY: Harper-Collins.

Fine, A. 1993. *The Angel of Nitshill Road*. London, UK: Mammoth Books.

Flake, S. 2001. *The Skin I'm In*. New York, NY: Corgi Books.

Hogg, G. 1998. *Scrambled Eggs and Spider Legs*. New York, NY: Scholastic.

Paterson, K. 2001. *The Field of Dogs*. New York, NY: HarperCollins.

Sachs, M. 1968. *Veronica Ganz*. New York, NY: Puffin Books.

Spinelli, J. 2000. *Stargirl*. New York, NY: Orchard Books.

_____. 1997. *Wringer*. New York, NY: HarperCollins.

_____. 1990. *Maniac Magee*. Boston, MA: Little, Brown.

Stolz, M. 1963/1991. *The Bully of Barkham Street*. New York, NY: Harper-Collins.

Scripts

Brooks, M., and M. Hunter. 1986/1995. *I Met a Bully on the Hill*. Toronto, ON: Playwrights Union of Canada.

Foon, D. 1993. *Seesaw*. Toronto, ON: Playwrights Union of Canada.

References

Beane, A. L. 1999. *The Bully Free Classroom*. Minneapolis, MN: Free Spirit Publishing.

Fine, E. S., A. Lacey, and J. Baer. 1995. *Children as Peacemakers*. Portsmouth, NH: Heinemann.

Fried, S., and P. 1996. *Bullies and Victims: Helping Your Child through the School Battlefield*. New York, NY: M. Evans and Company.

Heathcote, D., and G. Bolton. 1995. *Drama for Learning: Dorothy Heathcote's Mantle of the Expert Approach to Education*. Portsmouth, NH: Heinemann.

Paley, V. G. 1992. *You Can't Say You Can't Play*. Cambridge, MA: Harvard University Press.

Rigby, K. 2001. *Stop the Bullying: A Handbook for Teachers*. Markham, ON: Pembroke Publishers.

Stones, R. 1993. *Don't Pick on Me: How to Handle Bullying*. Markham, ON: Pembroke Publishers.

Assessment: Focus on Participation

Name: _____ Date: _____

Does the student ...	Always	Sometimes	Never
focus attention on the task at hand?	❏	❏	❏
follow instructions effectively?	❏	❏	❏
contribute ideas when planning?	❏	❏	❏
revise and shape ideas for presentation?	❏	❏	❏
accept different points of view?	❏	❏	❏
collaborate in a variety of group situations?	❏	❏	❏
appear to enjoy the drama?	❏	❏	❏

Comments:

_____

_____

_____

_____

_____

6/Folklore

We humans are storytelling animals. The drive to story is basic in all people, and exists in all cultures. Stories shape our lives and our culture — we cannot seem to live without them.

David Booth and Bob Barton, *Story Works* (2000, p. 7)

If human beings are essentially playful creatures then they are just as profoundly storytellers in the way they think and communicate experience. We communicate our daily experience to ourselves and to others in story form. We make sense of the behavior of others by inventing stories to explain why they act as they do.

Joe Winston and Miles Tandy, *Beginning Drama 4–11* (1998, p. vii)

· ·

Source: Traditional Tales

Theme Overview: *Once upon a time, the folktale was born. As these tales passed from generation to generation, some details were added, some forgotten, and some changed. In this dramatheme, students become part of this storytelling tradition as they go into the woods, make a wish, or discover the world that takes place in and beyond "happily ever after."*

Learning Opportunities
- To share personal stories and to listen to stories read aloud and told by others
- To explore the themes of folktales through retelling, storytelling, and improvising
- To tell stories with an awareness of audience both in and out of role
- To identify and explore the basic plot and central problem(s) of traditional tales
- To develop oral and written storytelling skills by elaborating and creating stories within familiar tales
- To practise revision and rehearsal skills in order to present work to an audience using Story Theatre and Readers Theatre

· ·

Games: Focus on Personal Narrative

Sharing Personal Memories

For this activity, students have a chance to share personal stories with half of the members of the class. They form two circles (an inner and an outer). Facing one another, partners tell something that they did during the past weekend. Some conversations may be brief; some will last a few moments. After a short period, students are given a signal to change. Members of the inner circle stay where they are, while members of the outer circle move one place to the right. It is up to the teacher to suggest conversation topics, such as an enjoyable movie, an embarrassing moment, or a favorite meal.

EXTENSIONS

- When students arrive back to their original partner, each partner exchanges stories that she or he heard.
- Students further practise their storytelling skills by retelling, in first-person voice, a story that they heard from a classmate.

Stories from My Past

Students work in small groups to tell stories based on a topic or question. They provide as much detail as possible and should be prepared to answer questions from group members. They can be given the list of topics to choose from, or you can assign a topic for each group to discuss. Suggestions are provided below.

1. What was your best vacation? Describe it.
2. Which teacher do you best remember? Why?
3. What was your most memorable birthday party? Why?
4. Have you ever been in danger? What happened?
5. When have you been afraid? Why?
6. What special toy(s) have been part of your life? Describe them.
7. What special accomplishment have you achieved?
8. Talk about the book that you remember best from your childhood.
9. Have you ever repaired anything? How?
10. Have you ever been admitted to a hospital? Why?
11. Have you ever had stitches? What happened?
12. Tell about a time that you had to move.
13. Describe a time when you were surprised.
14. Describe a time when you "learned your lesson."
15. Has a close family member or friend died? Describe the time.

Students are given a time limit to tell their story.

EXTENSIONS

- Choose a topic for the whole class to discuss. Students turn to others around them to share their stories. Volunteers can share their stories with the whole class. Sometimes, someone's story triggers other stories that students might want to share. Even though a story may not be on the original topic, that's fine!

- After listening to someone's story, students might work with a new partner or group and retell the story that they had been told.

Students take turns telling stories that come to mind when they hear one of the following words. Their stories can be about themselves, about someone they know or have heard about, or perhaps about books they've read or movies they've seen.

These words are story prompts:

lost	campfire	stitches
embarrassed	lonely	prize
accident	shopping	party
museum	seashore	contest

Memory Maps

Instead of using words to indicate important events and relationships, students prepare visual images that represent a "map" of their life. They draw images, people, objects, or symbols that represent memories. Although some writing may appear on these maps, it should be limited to single words or phrases. Encourage students to interpret the word "map" in any way. Some will represent images to indicate a journey; others will represent individual scenes to create a storyboard sequence of events. Students may wish to use magazine photos and captions to create a collage that represents their life.

Drama Exploration: Focus on Storytelling

It Could Be Worse
MEL: What a trip I had. First, I thought I lost my tickets for the plane.
BELLE: It could be worse.
MEL: The taxi got lost on the way to the airport.
BELLE: It could be worse.
MEL: I left my luggage in the taxi.
BELLE: It could be worse.
MEL: The plane was three hours late.
BELLE: It could be worse.
MEL: The stewardess announced that there was an alligator in the plane.
BELLE: It could be worse.

The students can continue "It Could Be Worse" with a partner or in groups. Each partner should have a chance to be the storyteller, Mel.

Students could play the game in groups of four or five. Each player could tell part of the story and add a detail that "could be worse" than the one before. Here are some suggested beginnings:

- Today I was late for school.
- Yesterday I was chased in the forest.

- This morning I lost my wallet.
- My sister was in a bad mood today.
- I was flying in a helicopter when it ran out of gas.

Students could also have each person alternate the storytelling with the words "Fortunately" or "Unfortunately." For example: A: *Fortunately, my lottery number was called.* B: *Unfortunately, I lost my ticket.* A: *Fortunately, the ticket was in my wallet.*

Tic Tac Tale Chart

A chart such as the following is given to the students, who work in groups of three or four. The students are told to select any three items that appear in a row (as if they were playing Tic Tac Toe). Once the group has decided which row to work on, members improvise a story that includes those three items in some way.

A magic coin	A princess	A forest
A unicorn	A wand	A giant
A fountain	An old cottage	A golden apple

Note: An alternative chart is available for this activity (see page 88).

EXTENSIONS

The following activities are alternative strategies for using the Tic Tac Tale Chart in a variety of group situations.

- Choose two rows to build a story.
- Act out the story that has been invented (e.g., tableaux, a two-minute improvisation, a puppet presentation).
- Present a story in mime.
- Each person in the group adds one sentence to build a continuous story; the group has two minutes to complete the story.
- Tape-record students' stories.
- Students make a chart with new phrases, e.g., toad/prince/castle.
- Students use their new stories as stimuli for writing original tales.

Story Wheel

This activity promotes listening skills and collaboration. Students lie on their backs and make a wheel formation, that is, their heads face into the centre. One person is chosen to begin a story. Each person, in turn, adds to it. The following phrases provide possible beginnings for the collaborative storytelling session:

- It was a dark and stormy night ...
- Long ago, in a kingdom far away ...

Tic Tac Tale

Work with some friends. Pick three pictures. Use the pictures in a fairy tale you create.

- Once, on the shores of a sea, a strange bottle was found ...
- He was always told to stay away from the door, but one day ...
- With a rub of the lamp, the genie was at last released ...
- Until today, everyone laughed at the idea of a time machine ...
- Once upon a time ...

EXTENSION

- The storytelling continues until someone interrupts and says, "Freeze!" That person continues the story, until someone else says "Freeze!" The activity can continue for several minutes.

Invent a Story

Students work in small groups to create a story, with each person contributing one word at a time to it. The storytelling continues around the circle until a satisfying ending has been reached.

PLAYER 1: Once	PLAYER 1: lonesome
PLAYER 2: upon	PLAYER 2: giant
PLAYER 3: a	PLAYER 3: was
PLAYER 4: time	PLAYER 4: wandering
PLAYER 5: a	PLAYER 5: through

EXTENSIONS

- Students stand in a circle and play the storytelling game with the whole class.
- The teacher tells the group that she is going to begin a story. For instance: "An ancient dragon decided to take a walk along the seashore one rainy afternoon." Each student in the circle contributes a sentence to the development of the story.
- Repeat the activity. This time, however, as each person "tells" the story, the rest of the group mimes it.
- Working in small groups, each student, in turn, adds at least one sentence that builds a story. The person on the right of the storyteller acts out the story that is told aloud.

Note: These storytelling activities could be repeated using a familiar fairy tale or after listening to a read-aloud.

Mystery Objects

For this activity, each student brings in an object (perhaps from home), such as a pen, a flashlight, a toy, a comb, a jewellery box, a bracelet. Alternatively, you or the students could bring in some unusual objects whose purpose is not readily identifiable.

Working in groups of four or five, each student is given the chance to create a story about the object being shared with the group. The story should give some importance to the object. Perhaps the jewellery box belonged to Queen Victoria, or the toy might have been the first one made by Santa Claus at the North Pole. Encourage students to make their stories as detailed as possible.

- Explain to the students that these objects once belonged to someone important who is no longer living. Each group should work to build a story about the person that incorporates each of the objects. Two groups could work together to share their stories.

Novel in an Hour

The class is divided into small groups so that each group is responsible for conveying important information from one chapter of a novel. Each group makes a decision about a strategy or strategies for depicting the plot and themes of their chapter. A humorous novel, such as *Sideways Stories from a Wayside School* by Louis Sachar, might be suitable for this activity. *Stone Fox* by John Reynolds Gardner and *Sarah, Plain and Tall*, by Patricia MacLachlan are also appropriate, since the chapters are not lengthy.

After preparation and rehearsal time, each group presents their chapter to the rest of the class. The chapters are presented sequentially to create "a novel in an hour" (or more).

Familiar Tales

Many children are familiar with such stories as Goldilocks and the Three Bears, Little Red Riding Hood, Cinderella, and Snow White and can appropriately enact the stories with their friends without much intervention from an adult. Traditional fairy tales, however, are rich for drama exploration that helps the students burrow into the meanings and themes of the tale. For example, Joe Winston, in his article "Emergent Writing and Role Play," describes his experience with young children working with The Three Little Pigs. The children were cast as the children of the village in whose neighborhood the story took place. Winston, working in role as Peter Pig, the youngest of the three brothers, sought help from the village children by explaining that he was jobless, homeless, and unable to read and write. Producing a letter that was "discovered" in the ruins of the twig house, Winston empowered the students to solve problems and to work beyond a plot that was familiar to them.

In their book, *Story Works*, David Booth and Bob Barton present four processes that have students work "Inside, Outside and All Around the Story."

---

1. **Enacting the Story** (representing what we have experienced)
2. **Elaborating the Story** (building on the story's strengths)
3. **Extending the Story** (stretching the story)
4. **Inventing from the Story** (creating new stories from old ones)

The following outline provides teachers and students with the experience of exploring a familiar folktale using these four processes.

Suggested Ways of Retelling a Story

- Chart paper: graph, list, summary
- Commercial
- Dance drama
- Diary
- Illustration
- Improvisation
- Interview
- Letter
- Monologue
- Movement
- Mural
- Overheads
- Poem
- PowerPoint presentation
- Props
- Puppets
- Readers Theatre
- Sound collage
- Still images presented in a sequence
- Storyboard
- Storytelling
- Storytelling in role (from the point of view of one character or more)
- Story Theatre
- Tape recording
- Videotaping

"If children are to learn from story, they must be able to express their individual personal concerns, ideas and feelings about it. The teacher's role is to promote thoughtful story response, to empower children to wander inside the story and wonder about it, making all kinds of meaningful connections."

David Booth and Bob Barton, *Story Works* (2000, p. 51)

PROCESS	FUNCTION		POSSIBLE ACTIVITIES
Interpreting the story	• express personal images and group images	TABLEAU	• create a frozen image to show the most exciting moment • add a scene before or after the image
	• review plot	STORYTELLING	• retell the events of a story from a character's point of view
	• depict narrative, images, and dialogue	IMPROVISATION	• enact a one-minute scene that demonstrates the dilemma/problem of the story
Elaborating the story	• build on the story using questions children might have	QUESTIONING	• draft questions as if media reporters
	• look for hidden truths	INTERVIEWING	• interview teacher in role as one who knows/might know • interview a character to find out the "true" story (pairs, small groups) • hot-seat to explore actions, behaviors, feelings
	• burrow into story to discover its theme	DANCE/DRAMA	• list words that express story's themes and create a dance drama movement (or dream) to express those themes
Extending the story	• explore what might have happened, or could happen before or after the story	IMPROVISATION	• improvise a scene to show what might happen at some past or future time

PROCESS	FUNCTION		POSSIBLE ACTIVITIES
Extending the story (*cont'd*)	• explore stories within stories	STORYTELLING IN ROLE	• brainstorm, in pairs, small groups, or as a whole class, a list of characters who could be telling the tale
	• work in role to experience problem in the story or explore unresolved issues	MEETING	• whole group meets in role to discuss alternatives/ solutions to a problem
Inventing from the story	• place characters in different situations from those mentioned in story by changing setting and/or time	WORKING WITH SET	• create a "set" for action to take place • improvise a scene to show how roles, languages, and problem would be different
	• use story concepts and patterns to create a new version	WRITING	• invent new characters, setting, time period, and dialogue to write a story patterned on the original
	• create a new story modelled on old by changing art form	PRESENTING	• Puppet presentation • Mime play • Videotape • Story Theatre

A Drama Structure: Traditional Tales

This unit provides students with several strategies for practising storytelling skills. A selection of storytelling and story building strategies are suggested for each of the four sources in this dramatheme.

Drama Convention: Storytelling

Storytelling increases students' mastery of language, showing them how words can be manipulated to make meaning and internalize language structures and styles. It develops the ability to turn narration into dialogue and dialogue into narration. Storytelling can provide the initial starting point for the drama; it can reveal an unexplained idea in a familiar story; it can focus details; it can serve as a review of what has already taken place; or it can be a way to build an understanding of a role.

Story One: Joseph Had a Coat

"Joseph Had a Coat" is a suitable story for storytelling, because of its repetitious pattern and predictability. A traditional version appears below.

Joseph Had a Coat

Joseph had a coat.
It was worn.
It was torn.
Joseph made a jacket out of it.

Joseph had a jacket.
It was worn.
It was torn.
Joseph made a vest out of it.

Joseph had a vest.
It was worn.
It was torn.
Joseph made a tie out of it.

Joseph had a tie.
It was worn.
It was torn.
Joseph made a handkerchief out of it.

Joseph had a handkerchief.
It was worn.
It was torn.
Joseph made a button out of it.

Joseph had a button.
It was worn.
It was torn.
Joseph lost it.

Joseph looked here.
Joseph looked there.
The button was lost.
Joseph had nothing.

So Joseph made a story about it.

This is that story.

Once the story is read to the students, they will easily become familiar with the sequence and be ready to retell it independently. Here are some ways to facilitate storytelling.

Cloze: Reread the story. Leave out words and have students join in to say the words aloud using the *cloze* technique. For example,

Joseph had a coat.
It was worn.
It was _____.
Joseph made a jacket out of it.

Joseph had a _____.
It was worn.
It was ____.
Joseph made a vest _____ ___ ___.

Picture Prompts: Let students work with one or two friends to retell the story using pictures. The students can decide how they will retell the story sequentially, as a storyboard or story map.

Sharing the Story: Students work with a partner. Each person takes a turn telling part of the story. The activity continues until the tale is complete.

Retelling by Clothesline: Students retell the story, making puppets or pictures to assist them in their retelling. They could use a clothesline to hang their pictures on as they retell.

An Interview with Joseph: One student volunteers to take the role of Joseph. As Joseph begins to tell his story, other members of the group interview him to find out more. The interview can be done in small groups or as a whole class of villagers who want to find out about Joseph's wardrobe. To prepare for the activity, students working in small groups could brainstorm questions that they might like to ask Joseph (e.g., What color is your coat? Where did you buy it? How long have you had it? Does anyone else have a coat like this?).

The Story behind the Clothes: Divide the class into six groups. Each group is assigned one of the articles of clothing from "Joseph Had a Coat" (i.e., coat, jacket, vest, tie, handkerchief, button). Each group is invited to create a story about the article of clothing (Why is it so special? On what occasion was it worn? Did anything unusual happen when the item was worn? Who saw Joseph wear this?) Once groups have prepared a story, have them share it with the rest of the group, using story theatre (narration and mime) techniques. These invented stories can become the basis for narrative writing.

Reading in Parts: Have the class read "Joseph Had a Coat" aloud by dividing the script and assigning parts to individuals, pairs, and groups.

Personal Stories: Prompt students to share stories about coats (or other articles of clothing) that have had significance in their lives.

A Meeting of Tailors: Ask students to design a new coat for Joseph. At a meeting of tailors, they can describe their coats and explain to Joseph why their design might be suitable for him.

Story Versions: The books *Joseph Had a Little Overcoat* by Simms Taback and *Something from Nothing* by Phoebe Gilman are versions of the Joseph story. These can be shared with the students.

Story Two: *Boo!* by Kevin Crossley-Holland
Retelling: Three or four students volunteer to leave the class. The teacher reads aloud a story, *Boo!* for example, informing them that one of them will be chosen to retell the story that they heard.

> **Boo!**
>
> She didn't like it at all when her father had to go down to London, and for the first time, she had to sleep alone in the old house. She went up to her bedroom early. She turned the key and locked the door. She latched the windows and drew the curtains. Then she peered inside her wardrobe, and pulled open the bottom drawer of her clothes press; she got down on her knees and looked under the bed.
>
> She undressed; she put on her nightdress.
>
> She pulled back the heavy linen cover and climbed into bed. Not to read but to try and sleep — she wanted to sleep as soon as she could. She reached out and turned off the lamp.
>
> "That's good," said a little voice. "Now we're safely locked in for the night."

Once the story is told/read, Volunteer 1, who hasn't heard the story, returns to the room. Someone is chosen to tell the story to Volunteer 1. When the story is finished, Volunteer 2 returns to the room, and 1 tells the story to 2. Volunteer 2 must then retell the story to 3.

At the end of the activity, have students discuss how the story changed from the first retelling to the last.

Variation: Arrange students in groups of about four. Two people from each group are removed as a story is told. As above, those who have heard the story retell it to someone who must then tell it to someone else.

Storytelling in Role: The next morning, the girl's father comes home and the girl wants to explain about the voice she heard when she went to bed: What did the voice want? What did the girl do when she heard the voice? What conversation did the two have? Working in pairs, students can improvise the conversation between the father and the daughter. Alternatively, the students in the class can collectively assume the role of the father and the teacher, in role as the daughter, can answer questions about what happened the night before.

Group Storytelling: Retelling in a circle is an effective way for students to reveal what a story or rhyme they have just heard has meant to them. No single student has the burden of the entire storytelling. As the story travels around the circle, each person adds as much or as little as they want to put the story into their own words. Participants can choose to pass on the initial round or so until they become more involved in the story. Using *Boo!* as a source, students can tell the story from the point of the father, the girl, or the voice.

Variation: The teacher can give a signal to change storytellers as the story continues around the circle.

Story Three: A Medieval Poem

In their book *Mother Goose Goes to School*, David Booth and Bob Barton describe their work with Grade 4 students responding to a poem by telling stories. Here is the poem:

> I had a little castle upon the seaside;
> One half was water, the other was land;
> I opened my little castle door, and guess what I found:
> I found a fair lady with a cup in her hand.
> The cup was gold, and filled with wine;
> Drink, fair lady, and thou shalt be mine.

Enacting the Story: Before they role-played, the class had focused on the term "lady" and decided that it would be a married woman. The words "castle," "lady," "thou," and "shalt" moved this story into a medieval setting. In particular, the students discussed their thoughts about the speaker of the last line, "Drink, fair lady, and thou shalt be mine." One by one, several children stood outside the door and knocked. When the door was opened, responding in role, they revealed different interpretations: a witch who offered a potion; a queen who had been deposed and wanted her power back; a knight who wanted to marry the lady.

Storyboarding: Give each student a large sheet of square paper, folded horizontally, then vertically to make a four squares. Have them illustrate one scene from the poem in each square. Numbered 1, 2, 3, or 4, students then meet in groups having the same number to create a story using their illustrations as stimuli for the storytelling.

GROUP 1: The story of the castle
GROUP 2: The story of the fair lady
GROUP 3: The story of the golden cup filled with wine
GROUP 4: The story of offering the drink

Story Theatre: Students work in groups to present a story theatre presentation, making decisions about narrators and action. Once stories based on the poem have been prepared, they can be presented sequentially.

Extension 1: Students create an illustration to represent a stained glass image that tells one part of the story described in the poem.

Extension 2: Students imagine that they have been hired by the king to tell stories at his next medieval feast.
a) Students can work in pairs, one being a villager who remembers the story about the fair lady who took a drink from a golden cup. They can decide whether the story was happy or sad. The storyteller can ask questions of the villager to ensure that the story is complete.
b) Students then switch partners. Those who were villagers are now members of the king's council who have been hired to listen to the stories before they are told to the king.
c) The stories are written down to be delivered to the king. Students can work in pairs to write the story "The Golden Cup."

> Drama Convention: Story Theatre
>
> In Story Theatre, the action and movement in a story are played out. The basic technique is that in addition to lines of dialogue/narration, students or a separate group of performers play out the action implied or described by the lines. Students can use the technique to work with a piece of text or a story that they created in the drama.
>
> Before interpreting a selection in Story Theatre, the group assigns roles. A narrator or narrators can be designated to tell the story, or the characters can serve as both narrators and characters within the story. When there are more roles than performers, some students can play more than one role. When there are more performers than roles, more than one student can play each role or portray an inanimate object necessary for the story.
>
> Story Theatre makes use of simple settings and properties. A coat, a scarf, or a hat may be all that is required in addition to ordinary clothing. Songs, sound effects, tableaux, and movement can enhance a presentation. Story Theatre is also a suitable format for older students to work with younger students.

Story Four: A Fable as Readers Theatre

The goal is to adapt a short fable as Readers Theatre, for example, The Frog and the Ox. To begin, students, working in pairs or small groups, determine which characters will be needed for the presentation of their fable. They then decide if a narrator will be used, and if yes, how many narrators will be needed. Alternatively, students may decide to assign a character to read lines of narration. Students practise reading the fable aloud to become familiar with both spoken and narrated parts. As students prepare the script, they should feel comfortable about eliminating, changing, or adding lines of dialogue to make their script read more smoothly. Bear in mind that it might be necessary to demonstrate to them how script dialogue differs from prose dialogue. Students might also make suggestions for the way that lines should be read and the way that characters should sit, stand, or move. They may also suggest gestures and expressions.

One way to determine whether students have been successful at script writing is to have groups exchange and read aloud one another's scripts. Stories can then be collected into a class script for others to perform.

The Frog and the Ox

A frog was sitting by the pond with his friends. They were all admiring a big strong ox who stood nearby.

"If only I were like that," he thought.

"Listen to him!" commented a friend from among the reeds. "All he can do is dream about being bigger than he is."

The frog was so small that the ox did not see him. But the frog, who could see the ox very well, was so amazed by his size that he almost died of envy. He puffed himself up as big as he could and asked the other frogs if he was now bigger than the ox.

"Not yet!"

The frog huffed and puffed and asked once more, "Who ... who is bigger now?"

"The ox," answered the friend.

Indignant, the frog tried again and puffed himself up still more. This time he puffed himself up so much that he actually BURST!

"You see," remarked the other frogs, "there's no way you can make yourself bigger than you actually are."

MORAL: Be yourself.

A Readers Theatre version of The Frog and the Ox follows.

Drama Convention: Readers Theatre

In Readers Theatre, a script is developed from material that was not initially written for performance. The techniques of Readers Theatre allow participants to dramatize narration and dialogue using selections such as fables. Readers Theatre does not require students to memorize lines, but before they read a piece aloud they should have an opportunity to think about and discuss the characters that they will interpret.

Choral speaking techniques can work very well in Readers Theatre. Timing and pacing can be as expressive as the sound of the readers' voices.

Readers Theatre can also be visual. For example, the group can create stage pictures or tableaux to enhance the script. Since listeners concentrate on the spoken word, gesture and movement should be used sparingly. There may be moments, however, when a significant movement by one or more characters heightens the dramatic impact.

In Readers Theatre, a decision needs to be made about how to present narration as well as dialogue. For instance, each performer might read lines of the narrator that describe his or her character's thoughts and actions, or, the narrator's lines might be read in chorus. The intent of Readers Theatre is to present a piece of literature intact, although all the words need not be spoken. If all words are included, some experimentation should be done with phrases such as "he asked" and "said the lion" that often appear at the beginning, middle, or end of a line.

Some Readers Theatre presentations can be made more dramatic through the use of masks or simple costuming, as long as they do not interfere with vocal clarity and projection.

NARRATOR 1:	A frog was sitting by a pond with his friends.
NARRATOR 2:	They were all admiring a big strong ox who stood nearby.
FROG 1:	If only I were like that.
FROG 2:	Listen to him! All he can do is dream about being bigger than he is.
NARRATOR 1:	The frog was so small that the ox did not see him.
NARRATOR 2:	But the frog, who could see the ox very well, was so amazed by his size that he almost died of envy.

NARRATOR 1:	He puffed himself up as big as he could and asked the other frogs if he was now bigger than the ox.
FROG 2:	Not yet!
NARRATOR 2:	The frog huffed and puffed and asked once more.
FROG 1:	Who … who is bigger now?
FROG 2:	The ox.
NARRATOR 1:	Indignant, the frog tried again and puffed himself up still more.
NARRATOR 2:	This time he puffed himself up so much that he actually BURST!
FROG 2:	You see. There's no way you can make yourself any bigger than you actually are.
FROG 1:	And the moral?
ALL:	Be yourself!

Beyond the Drama

The following twenty-five activities help students explore traditional tales through drama, talk, reading, writing, and art.

Dramatizing
1. Retell a tale in five frozen pictures.
2. Retell a tale as a dance drama (movement only).
3. Prepare a tape-recorded interview with a story character.
4. Create a puppet play.
5. Improvise a scene to show what happens to a character in the future.

Talking
6. Brainstorm questions that students might wish to ask a fairy tale character.
7. Conduct a talk-show interview with a story character.
8. Create a game show where questions are asked about fairy tales.
9. Have a story character party (consider costumes, food, entertainment).
10. Create an interactive folktale museum.

Reading
11. Create a bibliography of traditional tales.
12. Compare one or more versions of one tale.
13. Create a scripted version of a traditional tale.
14. Review a picture book version of a fairy tale, discussing the use of illustrations.
15. Adapt a version of a fairy tale as Readers Theatre.

Writing
16. Write and publish a modernized version of a tale by changing the characters and setting.
17. Write the diary entry of a fairy tale character.
18. Write a letter to an advice columnist in role as a fairy tale character.
19. Retell the story in poetry form.
20. Summarize the story in 100 words.

Creating Visual Art

21. Create a mask for a fairy tale character to be used in a story theatre presentation of a fairy tale.
22. Illustrate a scene from a fairy tale for a new published version of the tale.
23. Prepare a Wanted poster for an evil fairy tale character.
24. Create a sculpture of a fairy tale character.
25. Create a diorama that would represent the set of a fairy tale.

Recommended Sources

Andrews, J., and S. Ng. 2000. *Out of the Everywhere: New Tales for Canada*. Toronto, ON: Douglas & McIntyre.

Bruchac, J. 2000. *Pushing Up the Sky: Seven Native American Plays for Children*. New York, NY: Dial Books.

Crossley-Holland, K. 1998. *Short! A Book of Very Short Stories*. London, UK: Oxford University Press.

Datlow, E., and T. Windling. 2000. *A Wolf at the Door and Other Retold Fairy Tales*. New York, NY: Aladdin Paperbacks.

Falconer, I. 2001. *Olivia Saves the Circus*. New York, NY: Atheneum.

Gilman, P. 1992. *Something from Nothing*. Toronto, ON: Scholastic Canada.

Graham, C. 1988. *Jazz Chant Fairy Tales*. New York, NY: Oxford University Press.

Kushell, K. (editor). 2001. *Once Upon a Fairy Tale*. New York, NY: Viking.

Little, J., & M. de Vries. 1991. *Once Upon a Golden Apple*. New York, NY: Viking Children's Books.

Scieszka, J. 1998. *Squids Will Be Squids*. New York, NY: Viking Children's Books.

_____. 1989/1999. *The True Story of the Three Little Pigs*. New York, NY: Viking Children's Books.

Taback, S. 1999. *Joseph Had a Little Overcoat*. New York, NY: Viking Children's Books.

Thornhill, J. 1993. *Crow and Fox and Other Animal Legends*. Toronto, ON: Greey de Pencier.

Assessment: Focus on Storytelling Skills

Name: _____ Date: _____

Does the student ...	Always	Sometimes	Never
enjoy listening to stories read/told?	❏	❏	❏
share personal stories?	❏	❏	❏
enjoy creating stories?	❏	❏	❏
listen attentively to the stories of others?	❏	❏	❏
seem aware of audience?	❏	❏	❏
tell stories clearly with attention to sequence, character, and description?	❏	❏	❏
demonstrate an ability to retell stories?	❏	❏	❏
demonstrate an ability to tell a story in role?	❏	❏	❏

Comments:

_____

_____

_____

_____

_____

7/Community

When students take part in problem-solving experiences and have opportunity for choice, they make decisions and become more accountable for their own actions. They become more responsible.

Susan Schwartz and Mindy Pollishuke, *Creating the Dynamic Classroom:*
A Handbook for Teachers (2001, p. 4)

· ·

Source: Map

Theme Overview: *Whether we live in a small farming community or a large urban neighborhood, knowing the people around us makes us feel part of a society. In this dramatheme, students confront some of the problems that a fictitious village might face, in order to better understand the meaning of the word "community."*

Learning Opportunities
- To gain trust in working with others by participating in drama activities
- To create and interpret maps to convey information
- To invent a fictitious society and explore the issues and problems facing that society
- To select and develop a role in a problem-solving context
- To look at an issue from different points of view by assuming different roles
- To identify and explore the various people and places that contribute to a community

· ·

Games: Focus on Trust

Thumb War

Two partners meet as if to shake hands, but instead curl their four fingers and hook them into each other. Players stay connected in this way. The two thumbs are laid side by side and then switch places by jumping over each other three times. (Chant: *One, two, three, four … I declare a Thumb War.*) After they come to rest following the third switch they are ready for combat. The object of the game is to pin down the opponent's thumb for at least a count of three. The game is repeated until a person has won the best out of three matches.

EXTENSIONS

- Students exchange partners. Those who lost their first matches can partner with each other and winners can play winners.
- A tournament can be held until a Thumb War champion is declared.

Bat Cave

The class stands in a large open circle. One student, chosen to be the "bat," is blindfolded. Four or five students are chosen to be "moths." The remaining students in the circle form the walls of the cave. The object of the game is for the bat to catch, as silently as possible, a moth wandering about the cave. At any time, the bat calls out the word "Bat." The moths respond by saying "Moths." As the bat wanders around the inside of the circle, it might get too close to the wall. Students who are the cave wall call out "Cave." The closer the bat is to the wall, the louder the call. Once a moth is tagged, she or he changes place with someone from the circle. The bat, too, can change place with someone from the circle.

Obstacle Course

Students are divided into three groups. Group A creates a maze using furnishings and/or student bodies. Members of Group B must keep their eyes closed as they are led through the course by members of Group C. Leaders should be careful to lead their partners cautiously through the course by holding their hands and by making reassuring statements.

EXTENSIONS

- Every student should have the experience of being a blind person.
- The activity could be repeated by having the leaders use only verbal or sound cues without body contact.

Prui (PROO-EE)

Students gather about the room with hands outstretched so that they are not touching a neighbor. All players close their eyes, and one person is appointed to be *Prui*, the person who stands still and does not talk. The teacher can assign *Prui* by touching him or her on the head or shoulder.

On a signal, players move about the room with their eyes closed. When two players touch each other, they ask "Prui?" and if both have not been designated the *Prui*, they answer "Prui" and continue moving about the room. When someone makes contact with the designated *Prui*, that player remains still and silent so that the wandering person knows that he or she has found the *Prui* and attaches to him or her. The game continues as players search for the *Prui* and *Prui* grows. It ends once all players have found and become part of the *Prui*.

EXTENSION

- The game can be replayed with two or three people being designated *Prui*.

Crossover

For this activity a large space such as a gym or a stage should be used.

1. The class is divided into two groups. Each student should have a partner, although they will not be working together. Have the groups work at opposite ends of the room to create scenes that represent an image. One group will create a scene entitled "Peace," while the other group presents a scene entitled "War." (Another pair of words can be chosen to enhance a theme, for example, *urban/rural; chaos/tranquility; dream/nightmare.*)

    Each person in the group must be an element of the scene. The large group scene, however, may consist of a few small scenes connected together. Students should be allowed some time to prepare their large group tableaux, and then both groups simultaneously freeze into a position.

2. The "Peace" group remains frozen. The members of the "War" scene view that tableau, specifically for the positions that their partners have taken, noting the head position, the expression, the gestures, the relation to others in the group, etc. The "War" group then freezes into a tableau, while the members of the "Peace" tableau examine the frozen picture.

3. The members of the group then re-create the scene that they observed by assuming the positions of their partners. After a few minutes, each group freezes into its new tableau.

4. The two groups resume their original group pictures.

5. On a signal, all members of the group thaw out and move very slowly to the opposite end of the room until they arrive at a new position in the opposite tableau. The students are encouraged to move very slowly. (A piece of classical music will enhance the mood and movement of this activity.) The activity continues until both new pictures have been created.

6. On a signal, the students repeat the crossover by thawing out and slowly moving back to their original positions. The students may be asked to freeze at some point in the crossover. As each student is tapped on the shoulder, that student must call out a word or phrase that expresses his or her inner thoughts. Students can continue moving until they resume their original tableaux.

Drama Exploration: Focus on Role Playing

Experts

Students work in small groups. Each student, in turn, has a chance to become an expert in a particular field. The others interview the "experts" to test them on their knowledge of the field and their ability to answer questions. Interviewers could assume the role of an employment office. Working in role, students should be able to convince others of their expertise by answering the questions as authentically as possible. Possible expert roles:

- running shoe designer
- flea trainers
- window washer of skyscraper building

- circus performer
- moon explorer
- translator for alien creatures

Assign specific roles that can be used in a drama exploration, for example,

- a knight, to be interviewed by royalty that needs protection
- A "wolfologist," to be interviewed by a community that is afraid of the wolves who have been scaring little girls and little pigs
- an archaeologist, to be interviewed about someone who is writing history books
- an explorer, to be interviewed by the media
- an astronaut, to be hired by NASA for embarking on a new mission

Round Trip

The picture book *Round Trip,* by Ann Jonas, describes a journey from a small rural community to a big city and back home again. To help students consider the differences between an urban and rural community, have them work in pairs to role-play one or more of these situations.

- Two friends are planning a vacation. One wants to visit a big city for all the excitement, but the other wants a quiet holiday by a beach or lake.
- One neighbor went to visit a big urban centre and returns home to tell the other neighbor about the exciting trip. Stories are told about the sites, the food, the entertainment, the shopping, and a hotel.
- One neighbor makes a trip to the city, but finds it less exciting than anticipated. Some things happened that would make the person hesitate to visit the city again. Stories are told to the neighbor about the trip.
- An astronaut who visited a new planet returns home to tell the media about the experience.
- A family is making a decision about a place to move. Will it be surrounded by the jungle, atop a skyscraper, in the middle of a valley, or on an island?

- After role-playing the interview, members can write a letter, a postcard, or a travel diary entry to describe the experiences of visiting another community.

- Students work in small groups and prepare a comparison chart on what is good about living in an urban community and what is good about living in a rural one. The class can share their lists and take part in a survey to discover which type of living is more popular than the other.

Who Am I?

This popular theatre game encourages student interaction and role building. To begin, each student has a card that has been prepared with the name of a celebrity, a historical figure, or a novel or story character. A different card is pinned to the back of each player. Students are not to know their identity. The object of the game is for players to find out who they are by asking other players questions that can be answered only with a "Yes" or "No." They are allowed to ask one question per player as they wander about the room. Once players have guessed their identities, they pin their cards to their chests and continue to answer questions for players who have yet to discover who they are.

Note: To introduce the activity, you could assume the role of a famous person (e.g., Anne of Green Gables, Aladdin, Leonardo da Vinci) and have students interview you to determine the person's identity.

EXTENSION

- Students assume the identity of a character. With a partner, they can improvise one of the following situations: a job interview, an interview with an entertainment magazine, a telephone conversation with a friend, a conversation between two strangers who meet on a subway, and a conversation with someone at a party or wedding of a mutual friend.

Try to See It My Way

Drama allows students to examine problems from several points of view. The following activity prepares students to work in a variety of role situations, and encourages them to argue from different perspectives. Students work in groups to discuss one of the following problems. They are assigned roles and contribute to the discussion from the perspective of that person.

The meeting can be conducted in one of these ways:

Option 1: Each member of the group is assigned the same role (the whole class).
Option 2: Each group can be assigned a different role.
Option 3: Each member of the group is assigned a different role.

1. A new highway is going to be built.

- farmers whose fields will be destroyed
- city planners who must decide where to build the highway
- unemployed workers who will be hired to build the highway
- tenants who will be left homeless when their building is torn down to make room for the highway
- conservationists
- politicians who want to be re-elected

2. A tool factory is going on strike.

- employees who have worked all of their lives at the factory
- owners who must restrict their budgets
- clients who buy goods from the company
- workers who draw up a list of improvements
- safety inspectors who are dissatisfied with the factory's record

3. Space travellers are landing on a new planet.

- aliens who discuss the arrival of new citizens
- doctors who want to monitor travellers' health after someone has been taken ill
- travel agents who will advise the world about the discovery
- farmers who are inspecting the growth potential of the new planet's soil
- space photographers who have only three pictures remaining in their film
- movie producers who want to make a documentary about life on another planet

EXTENSIONS

- Repeat the improvisation. On a signal, everyone is assigned a different role and the discussion continues.
- The class meets together to prepare a whole-class drama where students deal with one issue. Each group presents different roles in order to fully examine the situation.

A Drama Structure: Map

Drama Convention: Maps

Maps are useful resources for initiating a drama activity as a focus for creating a fictitious setting, as a stimulus for inventing roles of residents living in that setting, and as a way to present, through diagrams, problems that may face a community. Similarly, maps can be prepared as part of the drama in order to reflect on experience and provide a symbolic representation of places, events, or periods of time. Students can also prepare a map of a community by creating a representation of a place they have read about in a story. Alternatively, they can make up a map and, as an ensemble, build a story, setting, and problem.

Phase One: Reading Maps

Students worked in small groups to discuss any information they knew about the community by looking at the map (see page 108). Before they moved into role, a whole-class discussion was held to determine what was known about the community. Questions such as these were asked:

- Did the map give you any clues about the jobs people had?
- Did the map show any special places of interest to visit?

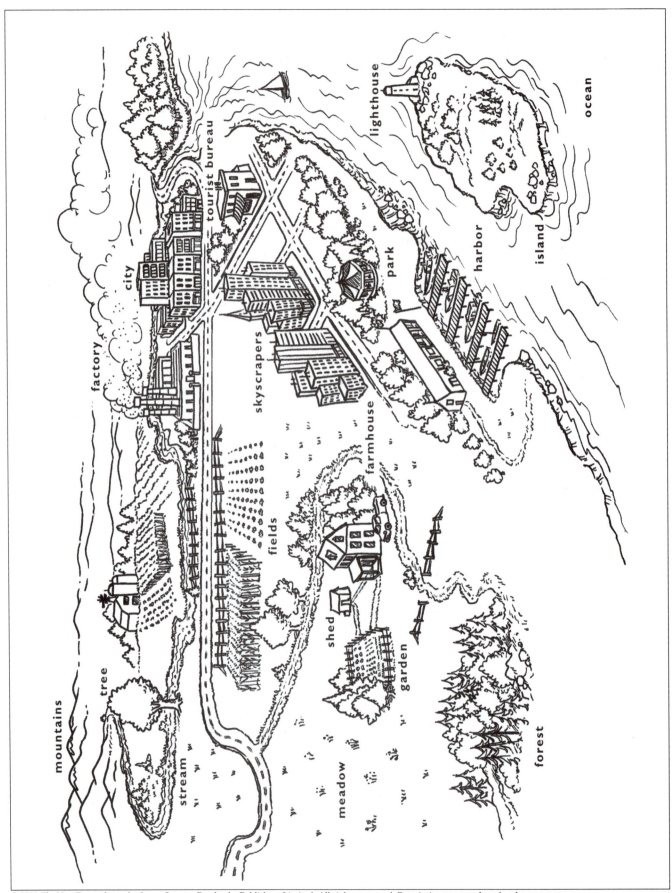

- How might you describe the community?
- What might be good about living in this community?
- What problems might this community have?

To prepare for the role playing, students brainstormed questions that they might ask citizens of the village if they were to visit there.

Phase Two: Interviewing to Develop Roles

Each student placed an X on the map to show where he or she worked or lived in this community. Students then worked in small groups to conduct interviews. One student assumed the role of a citizen while the other students played the role of tourists from another town who wanted the chance to speak with a resident about life in the community.

Once the interviews were completed, the tourists shared information that they had learned about the community. In role as the mayor of their hometown, I was given a summary of their findings and raised questions about interesting things they had learned about the community and about the people who lived there.

A discussion was held about a name that we could give to this community.

Phase Three: Discussing the Problem in a Town Meeting

Drama Convention: Teacher in Role

When a teacher works in role, she or he adopts a set of attitudes to work with the students. While acting skill is not required, the teacher must alter his or her status in the classroom to help students explore issues or examine possible directions that a drama may take. Depending on the role that the teacher takes, she or he can extend the drama, focus attention, challenge the class, suggest alternatives, support contributions, slow the action, and clarify information in order to enhance the commitment, the language, and the thoughts and feelings of students as they work in a fictional context.

To help the students consider the problem of the factory and the pollution it caused, I suggested holding a town meeting. In role as the citizens of the community, students gathered to discuss ways of dealing with the pollution. I assumed the role of an assistant to the mayor who arranged a meeting to listen to the concerns and problems that the citizens raised.

Students met in small groups to come up with solutions to the problem of how to deal with the factory's emissions. I then assigned a role to each group. In their groups, students discussed the pollution issue from these viewpoints:

GROUP 1: the unemployed
GROUP 2: mayor's council from city hall
GROUP 3: board of directors and owners of the factory
GROUP 4: environmentalists
GROUP 5: citizens who have lived in the community their entire lives

ROLE	FUNCTION	SOME OPTIONS FOR TOWN MEETING
Narrator	• shares memories of incident(s) • summarizes events, or action of drama	• citizen who "remembers the time when …" • storyteller explaining incident about the building of the factory
Leader	• establishes conflict, dilemma, and tension • challenges students to challenge, persuade, or resolve conflicts	• mayor of the community • boss/owner of the company • head of environmental committee
Opposer	• challenges decisions • disbelieves to demand proof, facts • opposes to bring group together	• developer who wants to build in the community • union leader who wants to protect factory employees
Low-status speaker	• elevates group's need to take responsibility • empowers	• factory employee • visitor to the community • potential immigrant
Messenger	• acts as intermediary • links authority and low-status roles • passes and/or receives information	• reporter seeking information • mayor's assistant who is compiling concerns
Shadow	• assists and side-coaches "in" the drama • shares commitment with children	• one of the concerned villagers • one who was born in the village long ago

Variations: Although the problem of the factory provides the central focus for exploration, other problems might be explored. Students may suggest problems that the community encounters once they have analyzed the map. These problems can be used to develop the improvisation. Potential issues include the desire/need of unwanted people to move to the community, the ambition of a strong individual to control the community, and the issue of destroying land to build a shopping mall.

Phase Four: Persuading through Writing

Students were given an opportunity to offer an opinion about what could be done to help solve the pollution problem. They chose one of the following contexts to persuade others to make changes:

- a *letter* to the mayor explaining how their life was affected by the decision to keep the factory in the community
- an *editorial* published in the local newspaper persuading readers to see their point of view and to take action to improve the community
- a *petition* to be drawn up and distributed among citizens that outlined community complaints, as well as suggested solutions/demands
- a *report* prepared by the factory owners explaining why the factory is beneficial to the community
- a "paid political" *announcement* to be read over the radio that advises others to take action

Once students had finished, they shared their writing at a press conference. Written pieces served as stimuli for further discussion, argument, and persuasion. Students discussed the possibility of compromise and offered hypotheses about the future of the community.

Phase Five: Back in Time
Students were asked to place themselves in the 1920s. Their town council had just received a proposal to build a factory. Their town, close to a large lake, has prospered on the summer tourist trade. The proposed factory would mean year-round work for the townspeople. Students wrote a letter to council outlining their support of or protest against the factory proposal. They later met with the teacher in the role of factory owner to discuss the issue.

Beyond the Drama

Planning for the Future
Students meet in pairs and revisit the map that was used to introduce the drama structure. In the role of land developers that have been hired to improve the community, they discuss how buildings, parks, stores, transportation, industry, and recreational facilities can be built to improve the community.

Following the discussion, two pairs work together and share their views. Each group of four then prioritizes the essential changes that they think should be made for the community's future progress.

Each group then creates a map depicting the community as it might appear in the future. They use chart paper to design the community as it will be 100 years from now.

Making Maps
Students work independently to create a map that shows the view from their window, the street where they live, and their home. Alternatively, they work in small groups to create a map that depicts one of the following:

- an ideal community that has no factories
- an industrialized community that has many new factories
- a community as it appeared 100 years ago

Representing Points of View

Students imagine that a local news program has been following the developments about waste disposal problems in their community. Working in groups of five or six, they prepare for a panel discussion to convince others to accept their point of view. Each group is assigned a role (homeowners, politicians, unemployed garbage workers, architects and engineers, members of the sanitation department) and discusses the issue from that point of view. One student from each group volunteers to represent their group on a panel to discuss the issue of how the problem of increasing garbage should be dealt with.

Making Laws

By making rules or laws, students create a document that focuses attention on specific problems, such as garbage disposal. They look at the necessity of such laws, what happens when the laws are broken, and what laws need to be modified to reflect changing times and attitudes.

Writing Letters of Justification

Students imagine that some citizens have chosen to move away from the community. They explore the scenario through hypothesizing about letters written by those who chose to stay in the community and by those who chose to leave. In each instance, community members (past and present) justify their reasons for staying or leaving.

Recommended Sources

Baker, J. 1991. *Window*. New York, NY: Greenwillow Books.

Barrett, J., and R. Barrett 1978. *Cloudy with a Chance of Meatballs*. New York, NY: Atheneum.

Blos, J. 1987. *Old Henry*. New York, NY: Morrow Junior Books.

Brown, R. 1989. *The World That Jack Built*. Toronto, ON: Stoddart Publishing.

Browne, A. 1998. *Voices in the Park*. New York, NY: DK Publishing.

Gantschev, I. 1985. *Two Islands*. Boston, MA: Picture Book Studio.

Geisert, B., and A. Geisert. 2000. *Mountain Town*. Boston, MA: Houghton Mifflin. (Also: *Prairie Town*)

Greenfield, E. 1991. *Night on Neighborhood Street*. New York, NY: Dial Books.

Hartman, G. 1991. *As the Crow Flies: A First Book of Maps*. New York, NY: Macmillan Children's Book Group.

Hennessy, B. G., and P. Joyce. 1999. *The Once Upon a Time Map Book*. Cambridge, MA: Candlewick Press.

Jonas, A. 1983. *Round Trip*. New York, NY: Greenwillow Books.

Mills, J. C. 2000. *The Painted Chest*. Reseda, CA: Tom Porter.

Snape, J., & C. Snape. 1989. *Giant*. London, UK: Walker Books.

Stewart, S., and D. Small. 2001. *The Journey*. New York, NY: Farrar Straus and Giroux.

Ward, H., and W. Anderson. 2001. *The Tin Forest*. Hampshire, UK: Templar Publishing.

Assessment: Focus on Role-Playing Skills

Name: _____ Date: _____

Does the student ...	Always	Sometimes	Never
recognize the difference between working in role and working as self?	❏	❏	❏
use language and gesture appropriate to the role?	❏	❏	❏
understand and identify with attitudes of the role?	❏	❏	❏
recognize and accept the roles of others?	❏	❏	❏
recognize and is committed to the intent of the drama?	❏	❏	❏
explain, question, and challenge in role?	❏	❏	❏
develop a character to build the drama?	❏	❏	❏
accept the teacher in role within a drama?	❏	❏	❏
reveal ideas and feelings in role through talk?	❏	❏	❏
reveal ideas and feelings in role through writing?	❏	❏	❏

Comments:

_____

_____

_____

_____

_____

8/The Past

Drama education is a practice that demands of the student an understanding of lived past experiences in order to inform the present.

Kathleen Gallagher, *Drama Education in the Lives of Girls: Imagining Possibilities* (2000, p. 120)

· ·

Source: Photographs

Theme Overview: *What would happen if we could use today's knowledge and apply it to yesterday's news? Stories about historical figures, explorers, pioneers, and heroes have always intrigued us. As we come to understand what happened before we were born, we begin to feel a part of the survival and quest of our ancestors. In this dramatheme, students look in history's rear-view mirror in order to be better prepared for the road ahead.*

Learning Opportunities
- To negotiate and cooperate with others in the development of drama work
- To practise role playing in order to better understand the thoughts, feelings, and motivations of others
- To use drama as a context for reflecting and writing in role
- To use writing in role within a drama context
- To modify and select vocabulary to suit different writing-in-role situations
- To research and use historical information arising from dramatic situations
- To examine the life stories and dilemmas of immigrants by working "as if"

· ·

Games: Focus on Concentration

Count to Ten

This activity, which builds group interaction and concentration, is not as easy to play as it may seem. Students sit in a group, or arrange themselves in a circle. The object of the game is to have the group count from 1 to 10, with only one person calling a number at a time. Students are instructed to call out a number when they think it is appropriate. The game begins with a student calling out "1." When two players call out a number at the same time, the game starts again.

EXTENSIONS

- Students count down from "10" to "Blastoff!"
- Students challenge themselves to count as high as possible.
- Students recite the alphabet.
- Students play games in pairs, then in smaller groups.

Wink

The class is divided into groups of seven or eight, and each group forms a circle. Everyone is given a slip of paper. One slip in each group has an "X" marked on it. The person who received the X-marked slip is the "magician" who performs magic by winking at another person in the group. The person winked at must count silently to 10 before announcing, "I've disappeared." If someone else in the group guesses who the magician is, then that person makes an accusation. If correct, the round is over, and the slips are drawn again. If wrong, the accuser must withdraw from the game. Can the magician make all but one victim disappear?

EXTENSIONS

- The game can be repeated by joining two circles together. It is recommended that there be only one piece of paper marked "X" the first time the game is played in a large circle. The game, however, could be played with two magicians. One magician cannot "zap" another.
- This time, the game is performed in one large group. Everyone draws a slip, but this time four or five magicians are at work. The students wander around the room. The game proceeds in the same way except that, if a person gets "zapped," he or she counts to 10 and then "vanishes" in a very dramatic way.

Three Changes

Two rows of players stand facing each other (or students can work in pairs facing each other). Each player is to observe the person opposite and to note dress, hair, etc. Players are then instructed to turn their backs. Each player changes one thing (e.g., removes a watch, unbuttons a jacket, reverses a belt). Players then face each other again. Each player must now identify what change his or her partner has made. If, after one minute, the players haven't guessed what their partners' changes were, have the students reveal the answers. Repeat the activity with players making two, then three or four changes.

Drama Exploration: Focus on Writing in Role

One Potato, Two Potato

This activity promotes concentration and invites students to pay close attention to detail. Each student is given a potato (or orange, or apple, or stone) to examine so well that they would be able to identify it in a mass of potatoes. Students are not allowed to mark their potato in any way. Potatoes are placed in a pile and mixed. Students must then find their potatoes within the pile.

EXTENSIONS

- Students write brief descriptions of their potatoes. A description should be detailed enough that someone would be able to identify the potato by it.
- Potatoes are displayed throughout the room. Descriptions are collected and distributed randomly throughout the class. Students are told that these descriptions have been filed with the police department under Missing Potatoes. Working in role as investigators, they try to match potatoes with descriptions.

A Historical Convention

(With thanks to Cecily O'Neill)

Prompt students to think of the name of an important or famous person from the past (e.g., Christopher Columbus, Gandhi). Tell the students to imagine that a convention of notables from history will be held and that each person is allowed to bring a guest to the convention.

On a signal, students wander about the room and introduce their guests to anyone they meet. At this point, they must exchange guests so that they keep the new guests until encountering another person. It is acceptable for each person to get a famous person more than once because he or she will have a chance to pass the guest on again.

Here is how the game might go:

JAY TO ED: I'd like you to meet Christopher Columbus.
ED TO JAY: I have Moses standing beside me and I'd like you to meet him.

Ed then takes "Christopher Columbus" and Jay, "Moses." Jay might then meet Barbara and would say, "Barbara, I'd like you to meet Christopher Columbus." Barbara then gives Jay her guest. After a few minutes, the teacher stops the activity and each person in turn tells who he or she *brought* to the party. The teacher then asks around the group to find out who presently has that guest.

To conclude the game, the students might ask questions of some historical figures they're not sure about.

The game might cause some confusion for some students the first time it's played, so it could be repeated in one or more of these ways:

- as a convention of heroes
- as a convention of celebrities

- as a convention of characters from novels (storybook characters)
- as an exchange of qualities that they think a friend should have
- as an exchange of "facts" they have researched, if the students are studying animals or countries

EXTENSIONS

- Provide each student with a file card or a small piece of paper. Invite them to write a short diary entry from the point of view of the character they brought to the convention (a hero, celebrity, historical figure, novel character, whatever).
- Once students have written their fictional diary entries, they can exchange them with a friend. Partners conduct an interview to find out more information about the character and deepen the role that has been assumed.
- The class decides on which two characters who were brought to the convention should meet. Discuss with the class which two characters would be interesting to put together, where they might meet, when they might meet, and how the meeting will develop. Two people can volunteer to role-play these characters and the improvisation can develop using a forum theatre technique, where the group offers suggestions about how conversation might continue.

Fictional Journal Entries

Writing a journal entry in the role of a character from a novel can help students understand how that character might feel about the problems, people, and events of the novel. Invite students to choose a character from the novel they are reading. Tell them to imagine that this character keeps a journal of events in the novel. In the role of the character, students write their thoughts and feelings about an event or experience. (You could provide file cards in order to encourage the students to be succinct.)

The journal entries might be made in any of these ways:

- at the end of reading a chapter or novel chunk
- after students have completed the novel
- as students continue to read the novel
- from different characters' points of view

Once they finish writing, students exchange entries with a partner and conduct an interview to find out more information about the story. One partner role-plays the novel character; the other partner, the interviewer, who assumes the role of the character's friend, parent, or teacher.

A Drama Structure: The Immigrant Experience

Phase One: Discussing Immigration

In small groups, students brainstormed reasons why people might move from one place to another. Students considered moves that involve short distances as well as moves from one country to another.

> ### Drama Convention: Writing in Role
>
> Drama can support writing activities, from reflective journals and letters to interviews and proclamations. It also provides opportunities for collective writing, in which groups collaborate on a mutual enterprise — cooperating in collecting data, organizing information, revising and editing — to be used in the subsequent drama work. If students are engaged in the expressive and reflective aspects of drama, living through the "here and now" experiences that draw upon their own life meanings, then the writing that accompanies the drama and the writing that grows out of it may possess the same characters and qualities.
>
> Writing inside a drama context, the students begin to think of themselves as writers, controlling the medium in order to find a way to say what they want to say to people they want to reach. Because writing may be used within the drama and may be read or listened to by others, there is a built-in reason to proofread and edit.
>
> David Booth, *Reading & Writing in the Middle Years* (2001, p. 102)

The class discussed reasons why people from the 1800s might have emigrated from Europe. The discussion was framed around the following questions: Why might people want to come to a land that was unfamiliar to them? What might they have to leave behind? Did they come by choice, or by force?

Phase Two: Writing in Role to Begin the Drama
Students, each given an information sheet (see page 119), were asked to imagine themselves in the role of an emigrant.

Phase Three: Using a Photograph 1
In this image (see page 120), two immigrants nervously watch as an immigration officer reviews their documents. Students could discuss what the family might be worried about and what questions the officer might ask.

Working in groups of three or four, students improvised a meeting between an immigration officer and those who want to enter the country. Using the profile, students assumed the role of immigrants and conducted an interview between one or more officers.

Following the improvisation, the teacher, as the chief immigration officer, listened to the officers about the people they met and a decision was shared about the success or failure of the people hoping to be admitted to the country.

Phase Four: Using a Photograph 2
Students examined a second photograph (see page 120) depicting many facial expressions of children leaving the immigration bureau to find their new home. They discussed the picture by considering who these children might be, how they are feeling, and what they are thinking.

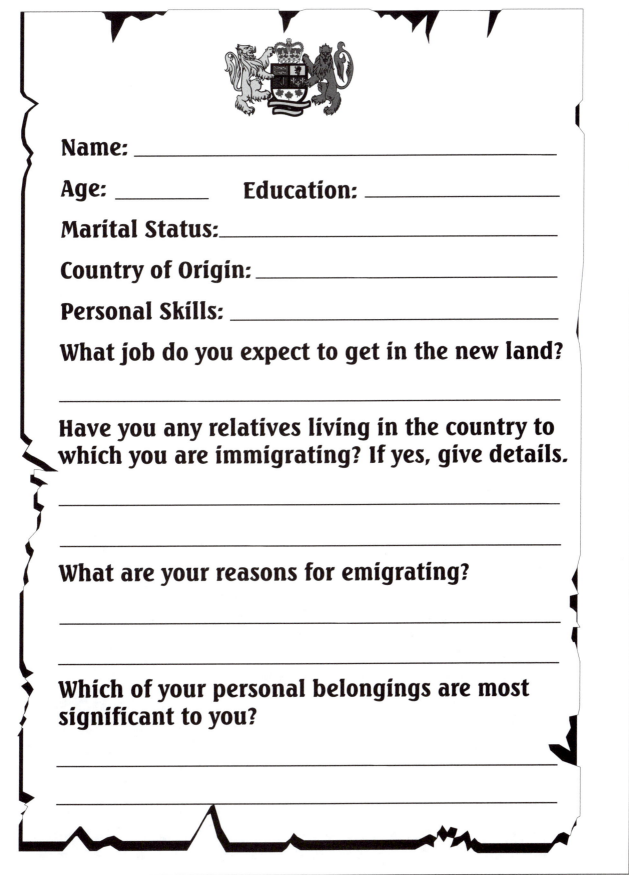

Name: _____

Age: _____ **Education:** _____

Marital Status: _____

Country of Origin: _____

Personal Skills: _____

What job do you expect to get in the new land?

_____

Have you any relatives living in the country to which you are immigrating? If yes, give details.

_____

_____

What are your reasons for emigrating?

_____

_____

Which of your personal belongings are most significant to you?

_____

_____

Using a Photograph

1.

2.

Working in groups of six to eight, students chose characters from this scene to portray. In their groups, they re-created the image as a tableau as accurately as possible.

The teacher instructed the students to consider what each of these characters was thinking. On a signal, each student revealed the character's inner thoughts by articulating a statement about his or her feelings and concerns.

Phase Five: Meeting with Officials

The teacher and a small group of volunteer students assumed the role of government land agents. A meeting was held with the students in the role of immigrants who had recently arrived in North America. The agents were offering free farm land on behalf of the government in order to settle sparsely populated areas of the country. The immigrants, however, were weary from their recent journey and somewhat skeptical about making another trip.

Prior to the meeting, the immigrants met in small groups to brainstorm questions that they had for the government agents (e.g., How long is the journey? What dangers might they expect? What kind of housing will they be expected to have?). Those role-playing the land agents brainstormed arguments for persuading the immigrants to continue their journey.

After the meeting, students, as immigrant groups, discussed whether they would make the journey to the farm lands.

Phase Six: Dreams

The class was divided into two groups to prepare dream sequences of an immigrant experience. The dreams could include speech, sounds, movement, and stillness.

Group 1:   Students prepared a dream sequence of the life that awaits them as they move to their new homes. They depicted their hopes and optimism about life in the future.

Group 2:   Students prepared images that depict the difficulties and hardships of coming to a new land (e.g., those related to equipment, health, terrain, and weather). What experiences, conversations, and feelings did they have to confront?

Once prepared, each group watched and interpreted each other's dreams. Alternatively, the students could adopt the Crossover technique (see page 104) as a way to contrast the lives of immigrants.

Beyond the Drama

The Planning Guide that follows provides possible contexts for students to write in role using this chapter's drama structure.

Planning Guide
Contexts for Writing in Role

- **Announcement**   An announcement inviting people to leave their homeland and settle in a new land
- **Fictional Biography**   A profile piece about an immigrant
- **Diary**   An immigrant's diary before, during, and/or after his journey
- **Interview**   A session between an immigrant and a reporter or historian to learn about the immigrant's experiences
- **List**   A list of pros and cons about moving to a new land
- **Letter**   Mail written to someone in the homeland
- **Monologue**   A personal reflection about life as an immigrant
- **Newspaper**   A media report on the progress of the immigrant's journey
- **Personal Narrative**   A record of a time when the student moved (*Note:* When done in role, such writing can be considered fictional autobiography.)
- **Report**   A progress report on how the immigrants are settling
- **Speech**   A welcome to new immigrants by the leader of the country/community
- **Song**   Lyrics that allow immigrants to reflect on their experiences; a song that could serve as their anthem
- **Petition**   A protest to the authorities about the poor conditions that new immigrants have encountered
- **Questionnaire**   A survey to be completed by those wishing to immigrate or who have recently immigrated
- **Transcript**   A transmission of an interview with or monologue by an immigrant

Recommended Sources

Aliki. 1998. *Painted Words: Spoken Memories*. New York, NY: Greenwillow Books.

Granfield, L. 2000. *Pier 21: Gateway of Hope*. Toronto, ON: Tundra Books.

Granfield, L., and A. Alda. 2001. *97 Orchard Street, New York: Stories of Immigrant Life*. Toronto, ON: Tundra Books.

McGugan, J. 1994. *Josepha: A Prairie Boy's Story*. Red Deer, AB: Red Deer College Press.

Oberman, S., and T. Lewin. 1994. *The Always Prayer Shawl*. Honnesdale, PA: Boyds Mill Press.

Ringgold, F. 1992. *Aunt Harriet's Underground Railroad in the Sky*. New York, NY: Crown Books for Young Readers.

Say, A. 1993. *Grandfather's Journey*. Boston, MA: Houghton Mifflin.

Yee, P., and H. Chan. 1996. *Ghost Train*. Toronto, ON: Douglas & McIntyre.

Student Self-Assessment: Focus on Writing in Role

Name: _____ Date: _____

1. Do you feel that drama helps you with your writing? Why is that?

2. Do you enjoy writing in role? Why?

3. How is writing in role different from other kinds of writing that you do?

4. What do you think is the purpose of writing in role?

5. What is your favorite piece of writing in role? Explain.

6. On a scale from 1 to 10, how would you evaluate one of your writing in role selections? Explain.

7. Did you share your writing with others? What comments did they offer?

8. How do you see yourself as a writer?

9. How do you feel you could improve your writing?

10. How did you feel writing this self-assessment?

9/The Future

We want a drama that enables children to make choice, decisions and to make sense of the worlds they encounter, yet we must also be mindful of the literacy learning to be delivered. When planning dramas, therefore, it is essential to get the balance right between the pedagogic and the fictional function of the work since they are interdependent. If the drama does not engage the children, the motive for literacy learning is lost; if the purpose of the drama in promoting literacy is forgotten, the drama may be valuable but does not deliver the required literacy objectives.

Judith Ackroyd, *Literacy Alive!* (2000, p. 4)

....

Source: *The Giver*, a novel by Lois Lowry

Theme Overview: *Only in drama can we turn the clock forward and make tomorrow come to life. Because no one can really be transported into the future, the students' ideas about the minutes, hours, days, and years ahead may be as real as those of scientists or the person sitting beside them. In this dramatheme, the students are invited to make predictions about life in the future and to share their concerns about a universe we cannot yet understand, but can imagine.*

Learning Opportunities
- To make predictions about life in the future
- To display imagination with conviction, concentration, and enjoyment
- To negotiate with others by playing games and participating in activities that involve collaboration and decision making
- To critique solutions to problems presented in drama and make decisions in large and small groups, defending their artistic choices
- To participate in and gain understanding of conflict presented within a novel by role-playing a central character in that novel
- To demonstrate the willing suspension of disbelief to travel to any place in any time
- To reflect on the meaning of memory

....

Games: Focus on Negotiation

Word Power
Students are asked to imagine that a wizard is about to take away all the words they know with the exception of three words of their choice. They record these words on a piece of paper. Students then use their three words to communicate with a partner. (They can also use gestures and mime.) To continue the activity, the wizard allows partners to share words so that each student adds three new words to his or her paper. Students find new partners and communicate with the six words on their list. The activity continues with students changing partners several times.

EXTENSION

- Students work in groups of six or eight. Members of each group decide on the words they would keep if the word wizard dictated that they could have only a ten-word vocabulary. As a whole-group activity, students decide on the ten words that they think are essential for communication.

Elevens
Sitting in groups of three, players chant "North/South/East/West," which is the signal for each member of a group to show any number of fingers from one hand. They count the total number of fingers shown. A closed fist counts as zero. The object of the game is for the group to show a total of eleven fingers. Players cannot confer with one another. As a competition, the first team to meet the object five times, or the team with the most number of successful completions within a given time limit can be declared the winner.

EXTENSION

- Players use both hands. The object is to show twenty-three fingers.

Furnishing a House
1. Working in their own spaces, students freeze into positions that show some piece of furniture or object that would be in the house, such as a chair, a lamp, or a computer.
2. The teacher directs students to create other pieces of furniture in the house, saying for instance:

   · Working alone, create a house lamp.
   · Working with a partner, create a house plant.
   · Working in groups of three, create a sofa or chair.
   · Working in groups of four, create a stereo system.
   · Working in groups of five, create a painting to hang on the wall.

   The students are told to remember who they worked with and how they made each piece of furniture.

   After the class has had an opportunity to practise creating various pieces of furniture, the teacher calls out the names of the furniture at random, and the groups re-form and re-create the furniture as they did before.

- Students can work in groups of six to eight to create frozen pictures that show various rooms in a house. Each group could be assigned a different room, such as the kitchen, the living room, or the bedroom. On a signal, have the whole class freeze into a picture to show the furnished house.

Machines

In this popular movement activity, students use their bodies to express ideas and collaborate to make a creation. Students are told that they are going to create a time machine. The activity begins when one student makes a repetitious movement that represents one part of a machine's engine. One by one, others join in, attaching themselves to the first person and to one another in some way. Each person, in turn, adds a movement. The activity continues until the entire group is connected and moving. On a signal, each person adds a sound to accompany his or her movement.

EXTENSION

- The activity could be repeated in small groups with each group creating a machine for the future that creates a product or performs a function beneficial to humans.

Soundscapes

With each student occupying a certain space, students interpret and create sounds using their voices, hands, or feet that describe

- falling rain
- a speeding motorcycle
- a winter storm
- a computer
- a haunted house
- a traffic jam
- a forest at night
- a storm at sea
- a robot doing chores

The students work in small groups and discuss the images that they thought of as they heard the sounds. The different sound images mentioned could be combined into a story about a future society. Each group prepares a soundscape, approximately two minutes in length, which may include words, song, and sounds made with or without equipment to convey life 500 years into the future. If available, students might use musical instruments to create their soundscape.

Groups can present their soundscapes to classmates who listen with their eyes closed and imagine the future world that has been conveyed through sound.

Drama Exploration: Focus on Problem Solving

Let's Not Argue

Although this activity can be done by having two partners sitting together, the following structure is a suitable alternative to help focus the students as well as to energize conversations.

Students form two lines, with each student facing a partner. Students in one line assume the identity of A; students in the other line assume the identity of B. Partners are assigned a conflict situation and a point of view. On a signal, each pair discusses the issue according to their roles. On another signal, students reverse roles to understand the other person's point of view. After a few moments, they switch roles again.

A wants to see a funny movie; B wants to see a horror movie.
A wants to play baseball; B wants to play a board game.
A wants to eat pizza; B wants to eat hamburgers.
A wants to vacation in the city; B wants a beach vacation.
A has a secret; B tries to get A to tell the secret.
A wants to borrow B's homework; B refuses.
A finds $10 and wants to spend it; B wants to find the owner.
A recycles garbage; B doesn't.
A thinks watching television is a waste of time; B is a television addict.

EXTENSIONS

- After each conversation, students can review arguments that they used and discuss the different ways that the roles were portrayed during the improvisation.
- On a signal, students in one line shift direction so that they have a new partner. They repeat one of the above situations and/or reverse roles.

Travel Time

"Oh, a time machine will never work —
You cannot solve its mystery.
So step right in," the professor said.
"When this button's pressed, you'll be history!"

"History be you'll, pressed button's this when."
Said professor the, "in right step so
Mystery its solve cannot you.
Work never will machine time a, Oh"

L.S.

Students read the poem to themselves before reading it aloud with a partner. They discuss questions they have about the poem and then improvise a scene between the professor and his "guinea pig." Who might be interested in entering the time machine? What questions might someone have before pressing the button? Will the professor convince someone to enter?

Partners then reverse roles. In this improvisation, the professor is selective about who he will allow into his time machine. What qualifications might this person need? How convincing must the applicant be in order to persuade the professor to let him or her use the machine?

EXTENSION

- Partners join with another set of students. Together, in groups of four, they discuss what might happen once the button is pressed. They create an image to show the period in the future that the time travellers have entered. Groups show one another their scenes as evidence that they have visited the future. Audience members, in role as the professor and his assistants, ask questions pertaining to the success of the mission.

Novel Openings

The excerpts below are openings to novels that are set in the future. Choose one of these excerpts to share with the students as a whole class or in small groups. Discuss:

- What information did you learn about the plot? character? setting of the novel?
- Which words or phrases have an impact on you?
- What questions came to mind?
- What do you think will happen in this story?

Arrange the students in small groups and give each group one of the openings to discuss. (Alternatively, students can choose to discuss a lead sentence from a novel they arc reading.)

> If you're reading this, it must be a thousand years from now. Because nobody around here reads anymore. Why bother, when you can just probe it?
>
> from *The Last Book in the Universe* by Rodman Philbrick

> She was with them only between the newing and the olding of the moon, but it was never forgotten, though spoken of secretly and in whispers.
>
> from *The Story Box* by Monica Hughes

> The Iron Man came to the top of the cliff.
>   How far had he walked? Nobody knows. Where did he come from? Nobody knows. How was he made? Nobody knows.
>
> from *The Iron Man* by Ted Hughes

> Far, far and jutting out in the emptiness beyond, like the figurehead of a mighty stone ship, is The Edge.
>
> from *The Curse of the Gloamglozer: The Edge Chronicles* by Paul Stewart and Chris Riddell

1. Provide each student with a file card or piece of paper. Have them privately write three questions that come to mind after reading the excerpt.
2. Group members share their questions.
3. The group negotiates the three most significant questions they have about the novel.
4. As a group, the students write a paragraph, using the lead sentence as a beginning, and imagine that they are the author of the novel. What information might they provide in the introduction to the novel? What language and images will they use to convey that this story takes place in the future?
5. Groups share their writing by exchanging pieces with another group.

EXTENSIONS

- Students raise new questions that have been inspired by the piece of writing they've read.
- Using the written piece as a source, groups create an illustration that would depict the setting of a future society.

Planning Guide

Web for a Source

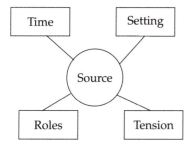

A Drama Structure: *The Giver* by Lois Lowry

The following events provide an overview of exploring *The Giver* by Lois Lowry (with thanks to Alifa R., Aivars T., Yana I., and Sharon S. for their ideas). The drama sessions can be used to introduce the novel, explore themes from within the novel, or reflect on the novel as a whole. If the students have not read the novel, they can be introduced to pieces of text as the drama develops. Alternatively, through drama exploration, students can probe some of the dilemmas and issues during their reading of the novel.

Below is a recommended graphic organizer for *The Giver*.

Planning Guide

Web for *The Giver*

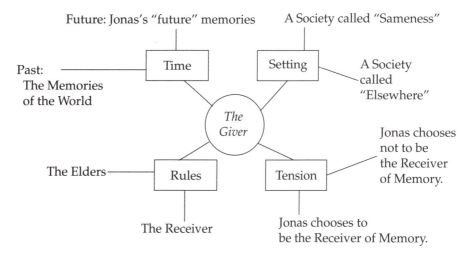

Session One: Introducing the Theme — Personal Timelines

One of the novel's themes is the preservation of memories. This introductory activity helps students to reflect on the memories and stories of their lives.

Students prepared a personal timeline by recording outstanding memories and episodes from their past. The timelines were drawn on a large blank paper (or a long strip of adding machine paper could be used) recording their date of birth on one end of the line and the present date at the other end.

The students recorded any details that they felt they'd like to present that would tell the story of their lives. The teacher explained that these timelines would be kept private if the student wished. The sorts of events that students included were moves to a new community, special teachers, vacations, prizes won, births and deaths in the family, accidents and illnesses, and special birthdays.

Note: The students may wish to mark off specific years on their timelines, although they may not remember much from their infancy. It is not essential that these events be recorded in exact chronological order.

Once the timelines had been completed, the students chose to share significant past events by working in pairs or in small groups. Timelines were shared with others voluntarily. A teacher or a friend asked some questions about a certain event that was recorded on the timeline.

Note: For more on personal narratives, see Dramatheme 6, pages 85–86.

Session Two: Introducing Jonas's World

The following book blurb, on the back cover of the paperback edition of the novel, describes Jonas's world:

> Jonas's world is perfect. Everything is under control. There is no war or fear or pain. There are no choices. Every person is assigned a role in the community.
>
> When Jonas turns twelve, he is singled out to receive special training from The Giver. The Giver alone holds the memories of the true pain and pleasure of life. Now it's time for Jonas to receive the truth. There is no turning back.

Students responded to that blurb in a whole-class discussion. They were then organized into six groups, with each group assigned a snippet of the text. Discussion focused on these two questions:

- What do you imagine this future society to be? Consider environment, government, employment, and recreation.
- What are the pros and cons of living in a society described with these words?

> GROUP ONE: Everything is under control. There is no war or fear or pain.
> GROUP TWO: There are no choices.
> GROUP THREE: Every person is assigned a role in the community.
> GROUP FOUR: When Jonas turns twelve, he is singled out to receive special training from the Giver.
> GROUP FIVE: The Giver holds the memories of the true pain and pleasure of life.
> GROUP SIX: Now it's time for Jonas to receive the truth. There is no turning back.

Groups then used these sentences as tableau captions. They created a frozen image to depict a scene from *The Giver*, as they imagined it to be. The students were told that this frozen image would serve as a model for a cover illustration of the book.

The student designated as "Jonas" in each group went to work with another group. The remaining group members worked in role as the Elders who need to make a selection for the next Receiver of Memory. The Elders question Jonas about his background and feelings to consider whether he would be appropriate as the "Receiver."

Based on the class's discoveries thus far, the students discussed what they knew, what they thought they knew, and what they would like to find out.

Circle of Life Sample Chart

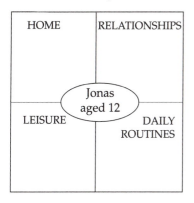

Session Three: Jonas's Dilemma

Using the drama convention called Circle of Life, students worked in groups of six to eight and developed a background for the central novel character, Jonas.

In each group, a large sheet of paper was divided into five sections, including a circle in the centre of the page. Within the circle, Jonas's name and age were recorded. The surrounding paper was divided into four sections, representing different facets of Jonas's life and the people he interacts with in the community. These were the headings.

Home: where Jonas normally lives
Relationships: friends and family (or estranged family) that Jonas might connect with
Leisure: hobbies, recreational activities, and social life
Daily Routines: habits? work? education?

The group brainstormed and recorded ideas about the character in the appropriate sections.

The following excerpt, introduced early in the novel, was then given to the students to discuss:

You will be trained to be our next Receiver of Memory. We thank you for your childhood.

On hearing the news that he was chosen to be the next receiver, Jonas contemplates what the selection means to him, feeling uncertain of what he is to become, or what will become of him. This inner conflict could be revealed in the context of Jonas meeting with other people in his life.

To facilitate this, the groups were divided into smaller groups of two or three. Each group took a different section from the Circle of Life chart and created a short dialogue between Jonas and other characters listed on the chart. The conversations focused on some of the thoughts, questions, and concerns that Jonas had about being chosen to become the Receiver of Memory.

Using the convention of thought-tracking, the teacher focused on different characters to represent their thoughts as they interacted with Jonas during the improvisation.

Drama Convention: Thought-Tracking

This strategy allows participants working in role to reveal publicly some of the private thoughts, feelings, and reactions of a character at a specific moment in the action. It helps them to develop a reflective attitude towards the action and to contrast inner thoughts with outward appearances or dialogue. Action is usually frozen and participants "tapped" to share their thoughts in role.

To conclude this episode, students discussed Jonas's fears about being chosen to be Receiver of Memory, his questions about his future life, and what happens if Jonas chooses not to be the Receiver.

Session Four: Jonas's Dreams

At the beginning of Chapter 5, readers are told that the family members in this society had a morning ritual of sharing their dreams. Jonas usually didn't dream very much and could seem to grasp only fragments of his dreams.

The students worked in groups to prepare dream fragments that Jonas might have experienced on the night he heard the news that he had been chosen to be the Receiver of Memory. The dreams were presented as a dance drama to the accompaniment of music. To prepare the dreams, students considered these questions:

- What story will Jonas's dream tell?
- Who will be in Jonas's dream?
- What activities may appear?
- What voices may be heard? Loud or soft?
- What sounds might be heard?
- What fragments of dialogue might be heard?
- How will characters move?

Once students prepared their dreams, they presented them to the class.

Session Five: The Memories of the World

In Chapter 10, Jonas has a meeting with one of the Elders where he learns more about his special selection as the Receiver of Memory.

> The man shook his head. "No, no," he said. "I'm not being clear. It's not my past, not my childhood that I must transmit to you."
>
> He leaned back resting his head against the back of the upholstered chair. "It's the memories of the whole world," he said with a sigh. "Before you, before me, before the previous Receiver, and generations before him."
>
> Jonas frowned. "The whole world?" he asked. "I don't understand." (p. 77)

In groups, students used a large sheet of paper to brainstorm significant moments in history that would comprise the "memories of the world." These stories could focus on particular people, places, or events and could include historical, scientific, artistic, or sports endeavors.

Students chose one event from history that they thought was memorable. They were told to imagine that television reporters were available for covering the event. Students prepared a two-minute news report or documentary telling and showing (tableau, dialogue, actions, interviews) this moment in history.

News reports were shown chronologically to show a history of the world. (*with thanks to Cecily O'Neill*)

Session Six: Jonas's Future

After examining the history of the world, students explored life in the future by predicting what would happen to Jonas. They worked their way through four phases. Consideration of the incident below led into the exploration.

The Giver gives memories to the one who is chosen to receive them. In the novel, Jonas receives the memory of snow and sled, the memory of rainbow and color. Jonas wonders why everyone can't see these memories and asks The Giver why color has disappeared.

> The Giver shrugged. "Our people made that choice, the choice to go to Sameness. Before my time, before the previous time back and back and back. We relinquished color when we relinquished sunshine and did away with differences … We gained control of many things. But we had let go of others."
> "We shouldn't have!" Jonas said fiercely. (p. 95)

Note: If the students have read the novel, this activity is appropriate for reflecting on the incidents and conflicts of the book. Alternatively, the activity allows students to predict what a future world for the character of Jonas might be like.

Phase One: Discussing Sameness
A discussion was held about Sameness. Why would people choose to go to sameness? Could this be a good thing or a bad thing? What could the people control? What would they have to give up for this sameness? Are differences good?

Phase Two: Developing Jonas's future timeline
The students were invited to go "forward and forward and forward" in Jonas's life and depict the memories that he will gain control of in the weeks, months, years, and decades ahead. They considered these questions:

> What will Jonas remember about The Giver?
> What will he remember about his family?
> What choices did Jonas have to make?
> Did he stay in the world of Sameness?
> Did he go "Elsewhere"?
> How will life change for him, as the future Giver?

Working in groups of three, students created a timeline for Jonas's life, predicting what would happen to him in the future.

Phase Three: Illustrating Jonas's future memories
Each student chose a memory from Jonas's future life. Using ordinary pencils or charcoal to depict the words without color, students created an illustration that would show Jonas's memories in the time ahead.

Phase Four: Interpreting the images
Students exchanged their drawings. Working in role as archeologists, they imagined that these illustrations were evidence of a unique culture in a different place and time. At a meeting of archeologists, students shared their "discoveries" and explained what they learned about the society depicted.

Beyond the Drama

Similar to writing in role, visual arts can be used within the drama to build context or have the students reflect on the drama. Students should have an opportunity to work in a variety of media, including paint, chalk pastel, oil pastel, charcoal, clay, construction paper, watercolor, pencil, marker, pencil crayon, photograph, and found materials. The following list identifies several contexts for using the visual arts inside and outside a drama:

- architectural drawing
- advertisement
- collage
- costume
- design
- diorama
- dreams
- map
- mask
- illustration

- photograph
- plan
- portrait
- poster
- prop
- puppets
- sculpture
- set
- sketch
- storyboard

Some possible art that is suitable to this theme:

Sketching Discoveries
Students are told to imagine that they can time-travel to spend one day in Sameness to experience Jonas's world. As evidence of their visit, they sketch some architecture, plant, house, playground, park, animal, person, or room that they witnessed. Once they "return," they can work in pairs to report their discoveries to one another.

Designing Images
The still images created for the activity "Introducing Jonas's World" can be used as a stimulus for having the students design a new book cover for *The Giver*.

Catching Dreams
In *The Giver*, the family shares their dreams. In order to help them remember them, students can create illustrations to accompany the storytelling. These illustrations can be used as a reflection of the drama work or as an alternative to creating a dance drama for the activity entitled "Jonas's Dream."

Creating a Portrait
Students create a portrait of Jonas in the future when he becomes The Giver. What clothing might he wear? What colors will be used to convey his personality? What images will be in the background?

Choosing Significant Memories
The Giver gives Jonas the power to have memories from a world that the young boy was unfamiliar with. As part of his training, Jonas accumulates more and more memories. Using images from magazines, students could create a collage of photographs to represent the memories that have been growing in Jonas's mind. They should determine how these images could be displayed effectively on the page and strive to choose images that have significance to the history of the world (people, objects, the natural world, events). They should be prepared to explain the images they have chosen.

Recommended Sources

Babbitt, N. 1985. *Tuck Everlasting*. New York, NY: Farrar, Straus & Giroux.

Fox, M. 1985. *Wilfrid Gordon McDonald Partridge*. New York, NY: Kane Miller Book Publishers.

French, F. 1983. *Future Story*. London, UK: Oxford University Press.

Hughes, M. 1998. *The Story Box*. Toronto, ON: HarperCollins.

Hughes, T. 1968. *The Iron Man*. London, UK: Faber.

Lowry, L. 1993. *The Giver*. New York, NY: Bantam Books.

Nelson, O. T. 1995. *The Girl Who Owned a City*. Minneapolis, MN: Runestone Press.

Paulsen, G. 1998. *The Transall Saga*. New York, NY: Bantam.

Philbrick, R. 2000. *The Last Book in the Universe*. New York, NY: Scholastic Inc.

Sadler, M. 1989. *Alistair's Time Machine*. London, UK: Hamish.

Scieszka, J. 1995. *2095*. New York, NY: Viking Children's Books.

Stewart, P., and C. Riddell. 1999. *The Curse of the Gloamglozer: The Edge Chronicles*. New York, NY: Corgi Books.

Assessment: Focus on Problem-Solving Skills

Name: _____   Date: _____

Does the student demonstrate an ability to ...	Always	Sometimes	Never
communicate?	❏	❏	❏
question?	❏	❏	❏
argue?	❏	❏	❏
persuade?	❏	❏	❏
negotiate?	❏	❏	❏
brainstorm?	❏	❏	❏
hypothesize?	❏	❏	❏
take risks?	❏	❏	❏
collaborate?	❏	❏	❏
reflect?	❏	❏	❏

Comments:

_____

_____

_____

_____

10/Diversity and Equity

When it is used as a medium for learning, drama demands no special space, materials or advanced techniques. It is a powerful means of communication, inviting argument and interpretation and acknowledging emotion. Drama provides a forum for exploration and expression, where growth in students' self-esteem occurs alongside the development of a sense of group identity.

Cecily O'Neill, "Aspects of the Process," in Anita Manley and Cecily O'Neill, *Dreamseekers* (1997, p. 85)

All drama involves some degree of audience in the sense that dramatic activity contains aspects of both creation and attention requesting of us that we watch others perform and/or be consciously aware of our own part in sustaining a fiction.

Jim Clarke and Tony Goode, *Assessing Drama* (1999, p. 83)

· ·

Source: *Skin*, a script by Dennis Foon

Theme Overview: *My blood is red. Your blood is red. Our blood is red. We are the same and yet different. By being invited to slip into the skins of others, students, in this dramatheme, may work together to gain an understanding of those who have opinions, values, cultures, stories, and "skins" both like and unlike their own.*

Learning Opportunities

- To explore a variety of ways that text can be read aloud, paying attention to subtext, characters, and setting
- To develop skills of cooperation by playing games and working towards presenting a piece of work
- To use script as a source for role playing and improvisation
- To use minimal scripts as a springboard for developing original scripts
- To produce work as members of an ensemble
- To contribute effectively to critical evaluation of their own work and the work of others using appropriate vocabulary
- To examine the concept of racism and stereotypes by exploring a script

· ·

Untangling

Students form groups of eight to ten. One member of each group is sent out of the room. Each group forms a line holding hands and, without breaking the handclasp, gets tangled up in the most complicated manner. When each group is completely tangled, the people who are outside return to their groups and attempt to untangle the bodies. Each "outsider" should untangle the group without giving verbal instructions. When untangled, people should be standing in the same line in which they started.

EXTENSION

• The group can tangle once again in a complicated puzzle. This time, group members should untangle themselves without speaking.

Discussing Values

The class brainstorms qualities that they think are valuable in life. These might be qualities that they admire in others or qualities that they think they possess, for example, honesty, intelligence, a sense of humor, curiosity, creativity, cheerfulness, optimism, perseverance, politeness, helpfulness, wisdom, charity, flexibility, and compassion.

Students receive three slips of paper each on which to record qualities that they would like as a permanent part of their characters. When finished, all slips of paper are put in a pile, and students choose three new slips. Students then barter with others in order to have the three qualities that they most value. Through the course of the activity, students may change their minds on qualities. The bartering continues for about ten minutes. On a signal, students keep the slips they have in hand, report those qualities to the rest of the class, and determine their level of satisfaction.

Finally, the class holds a survey to discover the most valued qualities and prioritizes those most essential to well-being.

On the Line

This activity helps students to build an appreciation of the opinions of others. To begin, an imaginary line is drawn down the centre of the room. One end of the line represents the position of "strongly agree"; the other end, "strongly disagree."

Call out a statement on an issue. Students move to a place on the line that expresses their opinion on the statement. The degree of support or opposition to the statement is evidenced by where students stand on the line. Students with no opinion on a statement stand at the line's centre. Encourage all students to express their opinions and not be swayed by the majority — they do not have to defend their point of view. From time to time, however, students may wish to express their feelings about a topic, or the class may wish to hold a spontaneous discussion on a topic of particular interest.

Here are some statements to present:

• It's important to study math.

- Learning to spell correctly is important.
- You should wear a piece of clothing because it's in style.
- Competition is good.
- You should never talk to strangers.
- School should be only four days a week. The length of the school day would be increased to make up for the missing day.
- Girls should be allowed to play on boys' sports teams.
- Honesty is the best policy.
- Cell phones are a necessity.

EXTENSION

- Students share their opinions on a controversial topic by having a panel discussion or debate. Once finished, they go back to the line to show the opinions.

Note 1: Younger students can play this game by expressing their opinion on simple topics, for example, red is better than blue, crayons are better than paint, dogs are friendlier than cats, and pizza is better than hamburgers.

Note 2: "On The Line" is a useful strategy to use in a drama where students give their opinions about a character's behavior or about a conflict that arises in the drama. Students return to the line throughout the drama to see how their opinions have changed.

Drama Exploration: Focus on Interpretation

Minimal Scripts
Students, with a partner, experiment with ways of saying the following lines aloud.

> I'll see you again.
>   Next week.
> Perhaps.
>   Very well.
>
> I'm sorry.
>   What?
> I said I'm sorry.
>   Sorry's just a word.
>
> What happened to you?
>   I'd rather not talk about it.
> Why won't you tell me?
>   O.K., but promise not to tell anybody.

As the following directions are called out, partners practise saying the lines of script aloud. In each pair, one partner takes the role of A; the second, the role of B. The pairs can practise saying the minimal scripts in a variety of ways:

- Say the lines as written.
- Reverse roles.

- Say the lines in a whisper.
- Say the lines as though talking on a telephone.
- One person says the lines angrily; the other, calmly.
- Both partners say the lines angrily.
- Pause for a few seconds between lines.
- Sing the lines.
- Say the lines quickly.
- Do an activity while saying the lines.
- Shake hands.
- Make no eye contact.
- Stare at each other.
- Sit back to back.
- Shout across the room.
- One partner shows no interest in the conversation.
- Say the lines sadly.
- Speak while playing a clapping game.
- Echo your partner's lines.

EXTENSIONS

- Students can prepare a short improvisation incorporating the dialogue while performing an activity (e.g., reading a book, playing with blocks, working at a computer, getting dressed, preparing breakfast, making a pizza, doing exercises).
- Students can improvise a scene using the conversations by choosing a role from column A and a setting from column B.

COLUMN A: *ROLES*	COLUMN B: *SETTINGS*
alien	in a restaurant
grandparent	in a cave
child	on the seashore
soldier	on a train
nurse	in an attic
principal	in a church
minister	in a graveyard
thief	in the library
dentist	in the sandbox

- Students continue the conversations by adding to the dialogue for a short improvisation.
- Students use the minimal scripts to end a conversation, rather than to begin one.
- Students write a short script by adding lines of dialogue to a minimal script. Pairs exchange scripts and prepare them for each other.
- Instead of working in pairs, students work in groups of three or four. The conversation/improvisation changes when more than two people are involved.

One Liners

Students work with one liners to begin conversations and develop an improvisation between two or more characters. As students work with any of the following one liners, they invent the characters and the situation that inspires the conversation.

1. Are you all right?
2. This is the last time I'm going to warn you.
3. May I come in?
4. I don't believe it!
5. Please accept my apologies.
6. Do you think you can keep a secret?
7. I don't know what you have against me.
8. What's your excuse this time?
9. Please leave me alone.
10. I don't think I can go today.
11. You're making a mountain out of a mole hill.
12. Where on earth did you put that thing?
13. Something should be done about it immediately.
14. Why can't you see anything from my point of view?
15. I'd rather not say.
16. How much did you say?
17. Shhh!
18. Are you still not ready?
19. Are you sure you have the right number?
20. Absolutely not!

Students experiment with characters, voice, and settings to influence the context for the conversations. They might use these strategies.

- With a partner, choose a one liner and discuss who might be speaking, where they might be, and why they might be having the conversation. The one liner is then used to begin a conversation.
- Instead of beginning a conversation with the one line, prepare an improvisation in which the one liner is the *last* line of the conversation.
- One partner chooses a line and says it. The partner continues it. Partners accept each other's responses even if they are thinking of different situations. The object is to carry on the conversation as long as possible.
- Experiment with ways of saying lines, for example, by raising or lowering voices, by stressing certain words, by using gestures, by changing eye contact, and by sitting or standing.
- Perform a chore while having a conversation (e.g., fixing a bicycle, making a cake).
- Work in groups of four or five. One person introduces a line to the group; each member finds a way to fit it into the conversation.

The Words of Martin Luther King, Jr.
When Martin Luther King, Jr., was growing up, he saw the WHITE ONLY signs throughout his hometown of Atlanta, Georgia. Haunted by these words, the young boy kept in mind what his mother told him "You are as good as anyone." In the picture book, *Martin's Big Words*, author Doreen Rappaport tells the story of Dr. King's life and weaves in the words and dreams of the great American.

Snippets of dialogue, taken from the speeches of Martin Luther King, Jr. (see page 143), can be explored with the students in one or more of the following ways:

a) Students read the list over and discuss what might have been the background for these statements to be said.

b) Individual students can share what they think is the strongest piece of text from the list. They can choose a sentence or a fragment of a statement to read aloud.

c) Students work in pairs to read one of the lines aloud.

d) Each pair can create a still image that would depict one piece of text.

e) With a partner, students create a scene in slow motion that would convey the message of the piece of text. They can then explore how to integrate the same words as they move.

f) Students create an illustration using paints, oil or chalk pastels, or construction paper that might accompany these words.

g) Students complete this sentence: "I have a dream …" to reflect on their personal hopes and wishes for the future of society. They could read aloud their statements individually or with a partner, accompanied by a still image or gesture. Students might rehearse a collective presentation of their scripted lines.

h) Invite the students to highlight the strongest words in each sentence. For example: It is ultimately more **honorable** to walk the streets in **dignity** than to ride the bus in **humiliation**.

These words can be arranged in an order, repeated, or added to to create a list poem.

i) The statements can be juxtaposed with another song, poem, or script. Here is how this might look with the script entitled *Skin*.

> I am five foot six inches tall
> *Everyone can be great!*
> I weigh 150 pounds
> *You are as good as anyone.*
> I have two arms
> Two legs
> *If we meet hate with hate, there will be more hate.*
> Two hands
> Two feet …
> *From violence comes violence …*

j) Using the themes presented in the words of Dr. Martin Luther King, Jr., students could work in small groups to produce an improvisation to show a scene in life that depicts racial tension, prejudice, or intolerance. As a further challenge, they could prepare their scenes in slow motion or stylized movement to the accompaniment of slow music. As students present their scenes, the words could be read aloud as a soundtrack to the action depicted.

Drama Convention: Soundtracking

Students can create realistic or stylized sounds to accompany an action or create an environment. Sounds can be produced using the voice, parts of the body, props, or musical instruments. Also, dialogue or text read aloud can fit an action that is presented by the students.

The Words of Dr. Martin Luther King, Jr.

We must not seek to defeat or humiliate an opponent, but to win friendship and understanding . . . every word and deed must contribute to an understanding.

If we meet hate with hate, there will be more hate. From violence comes more violence.

It is ultimately more honorable to walk the streets in dignity than to ride the bus in humiliation.

The strong man is the man who can stand up for his rights and not fight back.

Violence is immoral because it thrives on hatred rather than love. It destroys community and makes brotherhood impossible.

The ultimate measure of a man is not where he stands in moments of comfort and convenience, but where he stands at times of challenge and controversy.

Injustice anywhere is a threat to justice everywhere.

We must all learn to live together as brothers and sisters or we will perish as fools.

Everyone can be great.

Hate cannot drive out hate. Only love can do that.

Sooner or later all the people of the world have to discover a way to live together.

Wait! For years I have heard the word "Wait!" We have waited more than three hundred and forty years for our rights.

Love is the key to the problems of the world.

When we let freedom ring, when we let it ring from every village and every hamlet, from every state and every city, we will be able to speed up that day when all God's children, black men and white men, Jews and Gentiles, Protestants and Catholics, will be able to join hands, and sing that old Negro spiritual,
"Free at last! Free at last! Thank God almighty, we are free at last!"

I have a dream.

A Drama Structure: *Skin* by Dennis Foon

This structure focuses on the opening monologue from the play *Skin* (see page 145). Each scene in the play deals with a different aspect of racism or prejudice. Its effectiveness in promoting dialogue on these issues has been proved in countless classrooms, and its content and style make it an effective tool to use in drama exploration.

Session One: Oral Interpretation

Whole Class: To begin, students sat in a circle and read the opening twenty-six lines aloud as a whole class. Next, each student, in a clockwise direction, read aloud one of the lines. The activity was repeated by having students read the lines in a counter-clockwise direction. In this way, each student had the chance to read aloud two lines. Reading aloud in a variety of ways helped the students to understand that a line of dialogue can mean different things depending on the way it is read aloud. Meaning can be altered by stressing or emphasizing certain words (emphasis), raising or lowering the voice (pitch), and reading lines slowly or quickly (pace).

Students explored this minimal script by

- reading it aloud as quickly as possible
- pausing between the reading of each line
- reading lines aloud from a whisper to a shout and vice versa
- emphasizing one word in the line
- reading the line in a manner that was different than the way the last line was read, adding a gesture as the line was read aloud
- using gesture or movement only
- reading the piece as a round, that is, with one person reading from the first line — a few seconds later, the next person reading from the first line, and so on until each person had read the script aloud
- rearranging the order in which the lines were read

Small Group: To further practise techniques of interpretation, the class was divided into groups of four or five members. Each group experimented with ways of dividing the lines among the group. Some lines were read solo, some by pairs, and some by the whole group. Students were encouraged to practise emphasis, pitch, and pace. I invited them to consider actions and gestures that would complement or accentuate the meaning behind the words. As a group, they made decisions about standing or sitting, beginning or ending with stillness, and adding gestures as lines were read.

Extension: Groups then shared their rehearsed interpretations of these lines with one another. Each group was matched with another to present their piece and provided suggestions for revision.

Session Two: Improvisation

The class discussed the monologue in order to better understand the message that the playwright was conveying through the opening lines. The following questions led the discussion:

- What does this script make you think about?
- What message do you think the playwright was trying to convey in these lines?

Skin: Scene One

by Dennis Foon

I am five foot six inches tall.
I weigh 150 pounds.
I have two arms
Two legs
Two feet
Two ears
Two eyes
One nose
One mouth
Ten fingers
Ten toes.
I can taste.
I can smell.
I can see.
I can hear.
I can touch.
My blood is red.
My blood is red.
My blood is red.
My blood is red.
I breathe.
I think.
I feel.
I feel.
I feel.
I feel.

- Why would he use short lines and repeat some of these lines?
- Do you think some or all of the lines seem to apply to specific characters?
- What event might have prompted someone to speak these lines? In other words, what do you think happened to a character or characters that might have stimulated this monologue?

In small groups, students prepared a short improvisation to explain why someone might give this monologue that would serve as a preface to a play called *Skin*. In context of the theme of *Skin*, the improvisation would likely focus on an incident that depicts racism, prejudice, rejection, teasing, or bullying. To prepare for the improvisation, groups needed to consider who might have been saying these lines, how the person was feeling, where the lines might have been said, who would have listened to the lines, and what happened to this person.

Drama Convention: Overheard Conversations

This strategy allows students to work both in the role of participant and spectator. Usually, these conversations are not meant to be heard (e.g., spies plan a secret mission; a group of factory workers plan a strike). One strategy for eavesdropping on the conversations is to have groups freeze on a signal. Groups are brought to life one at a time to continue their improvisation. In this way, students listen in on conversations by various characters in the drama.

Once students rehearsed their scenes, each group got set to share its improvisation. On a signal, one group began, and when the teacher called "Freeze," the improvisation ended for that group at that moment. The teacher then signaled another group to begin, and the group continued until the teacher called "Freeze" once again. The activity continued as each group presented its scene. At any time in this process, the teacher can decide to return to a group which would then continue the improvisation about where it left off. The improvisation continues until the teacher calls "Freeze" again. In this way, the conversations go backwards or forwards to illuminate the situation.

Session Three: Hot Seating

Drama Convention: Hot Seating

In hot seating, a student assumes the role of a character (or someone who might know this character) from a novel, poem, play, or story or characters that have been introduced into a drama. When a person takes the "hot seat," that person is interviewed by classmates or group members who want to discover more about the character — how she or he feels about events, people, and places. Assuming the hot seat allows students to solidify their perceptions of a character.

In this dramatheme, hot seating was a useful strategy for having students speculate about the causes of prejudice and racism in some young people. In order to discover more about the attitudes and motivations of those who have caused trouble, several students volunteered to takes on roles portrayed in previous improvisations. They were hot-seated by the rest of the group about their attitudes to school, community, family, and so on.

Session Four: Preparing Minimal Scripts

Students worked in small groups to prepare an original script, that is, a short piece of dialogue that did not include notes on speakers and what prompted them to speak as they did. The intent was to make the dialogue and the situation as open-ended as possible. For this activity, the students prepared scenes that occurred before and after *Skin* was written. Groups exchanged their finished scripts and rehearsed the scenes for presentation. The scripts were then assembled to make a cooperative script called "Skin."

An alternative would have been to have two groups work together to share their presentations. Doing this increases cooperation as a number of students have to make decisions on adding or deleting lines from the script.

Beyond the Drama

Working with *Skin*

Students work with other scenes that appear in the script, *Skin*. Each scene depicts an aspect of racism or prejudice. Students practise ways of interpreting the scene by reading it aloud, and then create an improvisation that demonstrates the problem that the character(s) encounter. In groups, they prepare a presentation of the play. Given the script's open-endedness, several students can play the same character.

Creating a Collage

Using magazine or newspaper photos, students create a collage or mural that might be entitled "Skin." They also use words or phrases found in headlines or captions that could be suitable for use in their collage.

Writing a Monologue

Drama Convention: Monologues

A monologue is a short speech that a character gives to an audience. The character might use the monologue as a vehicle to express personal feelings and thoughts on a subject or event, or to tell a story or anecdote. Taking characters that they have role-played during an improvisation, students might draft monologues that convey their characters' feelings about prejudice. When finished, they read their monologues aloud to an audience (whole class or small groups). They should determine who the person would be speaking to and why. After presenting their monologues, students can answer questions in role.

Students can write short monologues by writing in the first person. They might use one of the following contexts: themselves, a character they have role-played in the drama, a historical figure, a character from a novel, a person featured in the news, or a character who appears in the play. Once the students have written their monologues, they might prepare them as list poems similar to the opening scene of *Skin*.

Creating Script from a Novel

Students can choose one or two pages of a novel they are reading to prepare a script. To help them choose an appropriate text, suggest that they examine sections with a significant amount of dialogue. They can make changes to the text, editing the narration and dialogue as necessary. Once students, in groups, have scripted a scene, they can prepare to present it.

If the class has read the same novel, each small group could choose a different excerpt from the book to prepare. Together, the class could work to present a scripted version. What follows is a conversation that appears on page 108 of *Trapped in Ice*, a novel by Eric Walters, and a sample script based upon it.

Michael started towards the ship. "I'll start eating, while you two talk."

"Where do you think you're going?" Mr. Hadley asked. Michael stopped in his tracks. "If you want breakfast it's being served in the big ice shelter at the end."

"Why can't we eat in the galley?" asked Michael.

"The ship's been abandoned. You know that."

"But you said it could be hours before the ship goes down. It won't take me that long to eat," Michael protested.

"Everything's been taken off the ship and onto the ice. Besides it could go down sooner, and when it goes down, it could go down fast," Mr. Hadley answered.

"Of course, Mr. Hadley," said Mother. "Michael, you must understand we're not allowed back on board. Everyone has left the ship."

MICHAEL: I'll start eating, while you two talk.

MR. HADLEY: Where do you think you're going?

MICHAEL: (stopping in his tracks) Why can't we eat in the galley?

MR. HADLEY: The ship's been abandoned. You know that.

MICHAEL: (protesting) But you said it could be hours before the ship goes down. It won't take me that long to eat.

MR. HADLEY: Everything's been taken off the ship and onto the ice. Besides it could go down sooner, and when it goes down, it could go down fast.

MOTHER: Of course, Mr. Hadley. Michael, you must understand we're not allowed back on board. Everyone has left the ship.

Recommended Sources

Adoff, A. 1982. *All the Colors of the Race*. New York, NY: Lothrop, Lee & Shepard.

Angelou, M., and J-M. Basquiat. 1993. *Life Doesn't Frighten Me at All*. New York, NY: Stewart, Tabori & Chang.

Avi. 1991. *Nothing But the Truth.* New York, NY: Orchard Books.

Bennett, J. (ed.). 2001. *Peace Begins with Me: A Collection of Poems.* Oxford, UK: Oxford University Press.

Bunting, E. 2001. *Riding the Tiger.* San Diego, CA: Harcourt, Inc.

_____. 2001. *Gleam and Glow.* San Diego, CA: Harcourt, Inc.

Bunting, E., and D. Diaz. 1995. *Smoky Nights.* San Diego, CA: Harcourt, Inc.

Craig, D. S. 2001. *Danny, King of the Basement.* Toronto, ON: Playwrights Union of Canada.

Ellis, D. 2000. *The Breadwinner.* Toronto, ON: Groundwood Books.

Foon, D. 1988. *Skin.* Toronto, ON: Playwrights Union of Canada.

Myers, W. D. 1999. *Monster.* New York, NY: HarperCollins.

Palomares, S. 2001. *Lessons in Tolerance and Diversity.* Torrance, CA: Innerchoice Publishing.

Rappaport, D., and B. Collier. 2001. *Martin's Big Words: The Life of Dr. Martin Luther King, Jr.* New York, NY: Hyperion Books for Children.

Raschka, C. 1993. *Yo! Yes?* New York, NY: Orchard Books.

Rochelle, B. (ed.). 2001. *Words with Wings: A Treasury of African-American Poetry and Art.* New York, NY: HarperCollins.

Smith, Jr., C. 1999. *Rimshots.* New York, NY: Dutton Children's Books.

Spinelli, J. 1990. *Maniac Magee.* New York, NY: Orchard Books.

Thomas, S. M., and E. Futran. 1998. *Somewhere Today: A Book of Peace.* Morton Grove, IL: Albert Whitman & Company.

Vaugelade, A. 2001. *The War.* Minneapolis, MN: Carolrhoda Books.

Walters, E. 1997. *Trapped in Ice.* Toronto, ON: Penguin Books Canada.

Wyeth, S. D., and C. K. Soentpiet. 1998. *Something Beautiful.* New York, NY: Bantam Doubleday.

Assessment: Focus on Interpretation

Name: _____   Date: _____

Does the student ...	Always	Sometimes	Never
investigate many possibilities of using voice to read the text aloud?	❐	❐	❐
experiment with gesture?	❐	❐	❐
explore various ways of moving, standing, or sitting?	❐	❐	❐
work effectively in role to interpret script?	❐	❐	❐
seem able to improvise dialogue?	❐	❐	❐
accept advice to improve the work?	❐	❐	❐
offer suggestions for shaping and presenting script?	❐	❐	❐
work well with others to explore scripts?	❐	❐	❐
seem to understand the author's intent?	❐	❐	❐
seem engaged with the activity?	❐	❐	❐

Comments:

_____

_____

_____

_____

Appendices

Recommended Resources by Activity

Games and Activities

Booth, David. 1986. *Games for Everyone*. Markham, ON: Pembroke Publishers.

Canfield, Jack, and Harold C. Wells. 1976. *100 Ways to Enhance Self-Concept in the Classroom*. Englewood Cliffs, NJ: Prentice-Hall.

Gibbs, Jeanne. *Tribes*. 1978/1994. Santa Rosa, CA: Centre Source Publications.

Maley, Alan, and Alan Duff. 1983/1997. *Drama Techniques in Language Learning: A Resource Book of Communication Activities for Language Teachers*. New York, NY: Cambridge University Press.

Rooyackers, Paul. 1996. *101 Drama Games for Children*. Amameda, CA: Hunter House.

Sher, Anna, and Charles Verral. 1987. *100+ Drama Ideas*. Oxford, UK: Heinemann Educational Books.

Movement and Dance

Grant, Janet Millar. 1995. *Shake, Rattle and Learn*. Markham, ON: Pembroke Publishers.

Joyce, Mary. 1994. *First Steps in Teaching Creative Dance to Children*. Toronto, ON: Mayfield.

Kaeja, Allen, et al. 1999. *Express Dance*. Toronto, ON: Dance Collection Danse.

King, Nancy. 1975. *Giving Form to Feeling*. New York, NY: Drama Book Specialists.

Landalf, Helen, and Pamela Gerke. 1996. *Movement Stories for Children Ages 3–6*. Lyme, NY: Smith and Kraus, Inc. (Also: *Moving Is Relating: Developing Interpersonal Skills through Movement*)

McGreevy-Nichols, Susan, and Helene Scheff. 1995. *Building Dances: A Guide to Putting Movements Together*. Champaign, IL: Human Kinetics.

Purcell, Theresa M. 1994. *Teaching Children Dance: Becoming a Master Teacher*. Champaign, IL: Human Kinetics.

Rooyackers, Paul. 1996. *101 Dance Games for Children*. Amameda, CA: Hunter House.

Shreeves, Rosamund. 1990. *Children Dancing*. East Grimstead, UK: Ward Lock Educational.

Walton, Rick, and Ana Lopez-Escriva. 2001. *How Can You Dance?* New York, NY: G. P. Putnam's Sons.

Out Loud: Chants, Choral Dramatization, Readers Theatre

Barcher, Suzanne I. 2000. *Multicultural Folktales: Readers Theatre for Elementary Students*. Englewood, CO: Teachers Idea Press.

Braun, Win, and Carl Braun. 1998. *Readers Theatre for Young Children.* Calgary, AB: Braun and Braun Educational Enterprises. (Also: *Scripted Rhythms and Rhymes* and *More Scripted Rhythms and Rhymes*)

Dunn, Sonja. 1999. *All Together Now.* Markham, ON: Pembroke Publishers.

Graham, Carolyn. 1978. *Jazz Chants for Children.* New York, NY: Oxford University Press. (Also: *Jazz Chants, Jazz Chant Fairy Tales, Small Talk*)

Miyata, Cathy. 2001. *Speaking Rules!* Markham, ON: Pembroke Publishers.

Swartz, Larry. 1993. *Classroom Events through Poetry.* Markham, ON: Pembroke Publishers.

Swartz, Larry, David Booth, Jack Booth, and Linda Booth. 2001. *Out Loud: Rhythms, Rhymes and Chants for Language Learning.* Toronto, ON: Lingo Media.

Walker, Lois. 1996. *Readers Theatre in the Middle and Junior High Classroom.* Colorado Springs, CO: Meriwether Publishing.

Story Drama and Role Play

Booth, David, and Chuck Lundy. 1985. *Improvisation: Learning through Drama.* Toronto, ON: Harcourt Canada.

Fox, Mem. 1987. *Teaching Drama to Young Children.* Portsmouth, NH: Heinemann.

Tarlington, Carole, and Patrick Verriour. 1991. *Role Drama.* Markham, ON: Pembroke Publishers.

Self-Assessment: Drama Reflections

Name: _____   Date: _____

1. Which game(s) did you enjoy playing the most?
   _____
   _____

2. Which drama activity/activities appealed to you the most?
   _____
   _____

3. Which do you prefer — watching others role-play a character or taking part in role play?
   _____
   _____

4. What does role playing teach you?
   _____
   _____

5. How does drama help you build your imagination?
   _____
   _____

6. How does drama help you to cooperate?
   _____
   _____

7. What advice would you give to someone who wants to take drama as a subject in school?
   _____
   _____

8. What did you learn about drama by participating in drama activities?
   _____
   _____

9. What did you learn about yourself by participating in drama activities?
   _____
   _____

10. What do you like most about drama?
    _____
    _____

11. What do you like least about drama?
    _____
    _____

12. What aspect(s) of your work in drama would you like to improve?
    _____
    _____

Self-Assessment: Drama Profile

Name: _____   Date: _____

For each statement, place a check mark in the column that you think best describes your feelings about working in drama.

		Agree	Neither Agree nor Disagree	Disgree
1.	I enjoy drama.	❐	❐	❐
2.	I enjoy playing games.	❐	❐	❐
3.	I enjoy working with different partners.	❐	❐	❐
4.	I enjoy working in small groups.	❐	❐	❐
5.	I enjoy working in whole-class activities.	❐	❐	❐
6.	I felt comfortable working in role.	❐	❐	❐
7.	Drama gives me the chance to share my ideas.	❐	❐	❐
8.	Drama helps me to learn how to solve problems.	❐	❐	❐
9.	Drama gives me an opportunity to deal with emotions.	❐	❐	❐
10.	Drama is for everybody.	❐	❐	❐
11.	Circle three qualities or roles that best describe your success as a drama student.	❐	❐	❐

- trustworthy
- cooperative
- confident
- imaginative
- curious
- playful
- conscientious

- leader
- good listener
- risk taker
- communicator
- problem solver
- believer

Put a check mark beside three qualities that you wish you had.

What does drama mean to you? Answer below.

_____

_____

_____

_____

A Rubric for Drama Participation

Name: _____   Date: _____

	Limited	Satisfactory	Good	Excellent
PARTICIPATION • appears to enjoy, and is committed to, drama • works well in a variety of groupings • investigates possibilities and contributes ideas • supports the contributions of others				
COMMUNICATION • communicates ideas and feelings orally and/or in writing • interprets ideas physically (movement, still image, dance) • adopts the attitudes and point of view of role				
PERFORMANCE AND CREATIVE WORK • uses a variety of drama conventions • selects, shapes, and presents ideas and feelings • is aware of audience, adopting appropriate tone and means of presentation				
CRITICAL ANALYSIS AND APPRECIATION • reflects on personal learning • interprets and analyzes the work of others				

A Rubric for Evaluating Role Playing

Criteria	Level 1	Level 2	Level 3	Level 4
KNOWLEDGE AND UNDERSTANDING	• demonstrates a limited understanding of the use of role to explore a range of perspectives	• demonstrates some understanding of the use of role to explore a range of perspectives	• demonstrates good understanding of the use of role to explore a range of perspectives	• demonstrates a solid and confident understanding of the use of role to explore a range of perspectives
COMMITMENT TO ROLE	• adopts the attitudes and point of view of role with limited ability	• adopts the attitudes and point of view of role with some ability	• adopts the attitudes and point of view of role with good ability	• adopts the attitudes and point of view of role with solid and confident ability
COMMUNICATION	• uses drama forms in a limited way to communicate thoughts, feelings, and ideas	• uses drama forms in satisfactory ways to communicate thoughts, feelings, and ideas	• uses drama forms in appropriate ways to communicate thoughts, feelings, and ideas	• uses drama forms in deep ways to communicate thoughts, feelings, and ideas
CRITICAL ANALYSIS and APPRECIATION	• reflects on personal learning in role to a limited degree	• reflects on personal learning in role to some degree	• reflects on personal learning in role to a significant degree	• reflects on personal learning in role to a strong degree

A Rubric for Evaluating Writing in Role

Criteria	Level 1	Level 2	Level 3	Level 4
UNDERSTANDING OF ROLE	• Thoughts, feelings, and attitudes of the role are limited.	• Thoughts, feelings, and attitudes of the role are satisfactory.	• Thoughts, feelings, and attitudes of the role are good.	• Thoughts, feelings, and attitudes of the role are strong.
REFLECTING ON THE DRAMA	• Reactions to events, statements, and issues in the drama are stereotypical or limited.	• Reactions to events, statements, and issues in the drama are satisfactory and somewhat detailed.	• Reactions to events, statements, and issues in the drama are appropriate and detailed.	• Reactions to events, statements, and issues in the drama are insightful and very detailed.
AWARENESS OF AUDIENCE	• Limited understanding of the context, function, and intended audience of the piece.	• Satisfactory understanding of the context, function, and intended audience of the piece.	• Good understanding of the context, function, and intended audience of the piece.	• Excellent understanding of the context, function, and intended audience for the piece.
QUALITY OF WRITING	• Format, language quality, conventions, and neatness are weak.	• Format, language quality, conventions, and neatness are satisfactory.	• Format, language quality, conventions, and neatness are good.	• Format, language quality, conventions, and neatness are excellent.

References

Ackroyd, Judith. 2000. *Literacy Alive! Drama Projects for Literacy Learning.* London, UK: Hodder & Stoughton.

Barton, Bob. 2000. *Telling Stories Your Way: Storytelling and Reading Aloud in the Classroom.* Markham, ON: Pembroke Publishers; York, ME: Stenhouse.

Booth, David. 2001. *Reading & Writing in the Middle Years.* Markham, ON: Pembroke Publishers; York, ME: Stenhouse.

_____. 1994. *Story Drama: Reading, Writing and Role Playing across the Curriculum.* Markham, ON: Pembroke Publishers.

Booth, David, and Bob Barton. 2000. *Story Works: How Teachers Can Use Shared Stories in the New Curriculum.* Markham, ON: Pembroke Publishers; York, ME: Stenhouse.

Booth, David, and Jonothan Neelands, eds. 1998. *Writing in Role: Classroom Projects Connecting Writing and Drama.* Hamilton, ON: Caliburn Enterprises.

Brown, Victoria, and Sarah Pleydell. 1999. *The Dramatic Difference.* Portsmouth, NH: Heinemann.

Clarke, Jim, and Tony Goode. 1999. *Assessing Drama.* London, UK: National Drama Publications.

Engel, Susan. 1995. *The Stories Children Tell: Making Sense of the Narratives of Childhood.* New York, NY: W. H. Freeman.

Gallagher, Kathleen. 2000. *Drama Education in the Lives of Girls: Imagining Possibilities.* Toronto, ON: University of Toronto Press.

Heathcote, Dorothy, and Gavin Bolton. 1995. *Drama for Learning: Dorothy Heathcote's Mantle of the Expert Approach to Education.* Portsmouth, NH: Heinemann.

Johnson, Liz, and Cecily O'Neill. 1984. *Dorothy Heathcote: Collected Writings on Education and Drama.* London, UK: Hutchinson.

Manley, Anita, and Cecily O'Neill, eds. 1997. *Dreamseekers: Creative Approaches to the African American Heritage.* Portsmouth, NH: Heinemann.

McLeod, John. 1988. *Drama Is Real Pretending.* Victoria, Australia: Ministry of Education (Schools Division).

Mearns, Hughes. 1929/1958. *Creative Power.* New York, NY: Dover Publications.

Morgan, Norah, and Juliana Saxton. 1994. *Asking Better Questions.* Markham, ON: Pembroke Publishers.

Neelands, Jonothan. 1998. *Beginning Drama, 11–14.* London, UK: David Fulton Publishers.

Neelands, Jonothan, and Tony Goode. 1990/2000. *Structuring Drama Work: A Handbook of Available Forms in Theatre and Drama.* 2d ed. New York, NY: Cambridge University Press.

O'Neill, Cecily, and Allan Lambert. 1982. *Drama Structures: A Practical Handbook for Teachers.* London, UK: Hutchinson.

Paley, Vivian Gussin. 1993. *You Can't Say You Can't Play.* Cambridge, MA: Harvard University Press.

Pitman, Walter. 1999. *Learning the Arts in an Age of Uncertainty.* Toronto, ON: Arts Education Council of Ontario.

Schwartz, Susan, and Mindy Pollishuke. 2001. *Creating the Dynamic Classroom: A Handbook for Teachers.* Toronto, ON: Irwin Publishing.

Taylor, Philip. 2000. *The Drama Classroom: Action, Reflection and Transformation.* New York, NY: Routledge Farmer.

Toye, Nigel, and Francis Prendiville. 2000. *Drama and Traditional Story for the Early Years.* New York, NY: Routledge Farmer.

Wagner, Betty Jane. 1976/1999. *Dorothy Heathcote: Drama as a Learning Medium.* Portland, ME: Calendar Island Publishers.

Winston, Joe, and Miles Tandy. 1998. *Beginning Drama 4–11.* London, UK: David Fulton Publishers.

Index